HEART ESSENCE *of the* KHANDRO

EXPERIENTIAL INSTRUCTIONS ON BÖNPO DZOGCHEN:

Thirty Signs and Meanings from Women Lineage-Holders

HERITAGE PUBLISHERS
19-A, Ansari Road, Daryaganj,
New Delhi - 110 002

Cover and book design by Dmitry Ermakov
Thangka by Pönzang Geshe Mönlam Wangyal
Digital imaging correction by Richard Williamson

HERITAGE PUBLISHERS

19-A, Ansari Road, Daryaganj,
New Delhi - 110 002
Tel.: 23266258, 23264444
Fax.: 23263050
E-mail: info@heritagepublishers.in

ISBN: 978-81-7026-282-4

Printed in India

Sagar Printers, 23 Ansari Road,
New Delhi - 110 002

The Cycle of Essential Dzogchen Instructions from the Male and Female Lineages of Yetri Thasel

Teachings by Yongdzin Lopön Tenzin Namdak Rinpoche on

སྤྱི་རྒྱུད་ཆེན་པོ་ནམ་མཁའ་དཀར་པོ་ཡེ་ཁྲི་མཐའ་སེལ་ལས་ཕོ་བརྒྱུད་དང་མོ་བརྒྱུད་གཉིས་ཀྱི་
དོན་གྱི་གདམས་སྐོར་ལས་མོ་བརྒྱུད་བརྡ་དོན་སུམ་ཅུ་པ་བཞུགས་སོ།།

རྫོགས་ཆེན་ཡེ་ཁྲིའི་བརྒྱུད་རིམ་མཁའ་འགྲོའི་ཚོགས་ཀྱི་བཀོད་པ།།

The arrangement of the Khandro Mogyud Lineage for the Thangka

Compiled by Yongdzin Lopön Tenzin Namdak Rinpoche

Translated by Nagru Geshe Gelek Jinpa, Carol Ermakova and Dmitry Ermakov

སྤྱི་རྒྱུད་ཆེན་པོ་ནམ་མཁའ་དཀར་པོ་ཡེ་ཁྲི་མཐའ་སེལ་ལས་ཕོ་བརྒྱུད་དང་མོ་བརྒྱུད་གཉིས་ཀྱི་
དོན་གྱི་གདམས་སྐོར་ལས་མོ་བརྒྱུད་བརྡ་དོན་སུམ་ཅུ་པ་བཞུགས་སོ།།

Thirty Signs and Meanings of the Female Lineage,
From The Cycle of Essential Instructions of the Male and Female Lineages,
From The Great General Tantra, White Sky: Liberating Extremes of the Mind

Recorded by Drenpa Namkha

Translation of the root text by
Nagru Geshe Gelek Jinpa, Carol Ermakova and Dmitry Ermakov

མཁའ་འགྲོ་ཅོ་ཟ་བོན་མོའི་གསོལ་འདེབས།

Prayer to Khandro Chöza Bönmo

Translated by Nagru Geshe Gelek Jinpa, Carol Ermakova and Dmitry Ermakov

མཁའ་འགྲོ་ཅོ་ཟ་བོན་མོའི་རྣམ་ཐར་སྐལ་ལྡན་སེམས་ཀྱི་སྒྲོན་མེ།།

The Lamp of the Fortunate Mind
A hagiography of Khandro Chöza Bönmo

Compiled by Nagru Geshe Gelek Jinpa

Translated by Nagru Geshe Gelek Jinpa, Carol Ermakova and Dmitry Ermakov

ལྷ་ཆེན་དྲན་པ་ནམ་མཁའི་གསོལ་འདེབས་བཞུགས་སོ། སྤྲུལ་སྐུ་བློ་ལྡན་སྙིང་པོའི་སྙན་རྒྱུད། སྨན་རིའི་ཡོངས་འཛིན་སློབ་དཔོན་སངས་རྒྱས་
བསྟན་འཛིན་གྱིས་དྲན་པའི་ཁ་བྱང་ལས་ཟུར་དུ་ཕྱུང་པའོ།།

Prayer to Lachen Drenpa Namkha from the Oral Tradition of Trulku Loden Nyingpo
Drawn from Drenpa Namkha's Prophetic Sayings by Menri Yongdzin Lopön Sanggye Tenzin

Orally translated by Yongdzin Lopön Tenzin Namdak Rinpoche

Edited by Khenpo Tenpa Yungdrung, Carol Ermakova and Dmitry Ermakov

CONTENTS

FOREWORD

PREFACE

ACKNOWLEDGEMENTS

THE KHANDRO CYCLE OF MOGYUD: Spelling, Transliteration and Translation of the Names....19

THE ARRANGEMENT OF THE KHANDRO MOGYUD LINEAGE FOR THE THANGKA....23

རྫོགས་ཆེན་ཡེ་ཁྲིའི་བརྒྱུད་རིམ་མཁའ་འགྲོའི་ཚོགས་ཀྱི་བཀོད་པ་ཡེ་ཁྲིའི་མཁའ་འགྲོ་མོ་བརྒྱུད་ཀྱི་ལེའུ་བཞུགས་སོ།།....29

THE CYCLE OF Essential DZOGCHEN INSTRUCTIONS FROM THE MALE AND FEMALE LINEAGES OF YETRI THASEL: Teachings by Yongdzin Lopön Tenzin Namdak Rinpoche....33

Preliminary Comments....33

The origin of suffering and the way to purify it..33

Kunzhi Namshe....34

Four points regarding collecting karmic causes....35

The Suffering of Humans....37

The summary of the View from the Male Lineage....39

Three Drenpa Namkhas....39

Guru Yoga with Drenpa Namkha....40

Introduction to the Natural State....41

Meditation....42

Integrating meditation with activities....44

Empty Form..47

Dzogchen, Refuge and Bodhichitta....................48

Thirty Signs and Meanings of Mogyud, the Female Lineage..50

Khandro Yoga..**52**

Body posture..52

Visualization..52

1. Dzema Yiwongma..54

2. Gyagar Khandro Ulishak..............................54

3. Walmoza Namkha Wökyi Gyalmo................56

4. Razhagza Salwa Yingchyugma......................58

5. Zhangzhungza Wökyi Lama.........................60

6. Dongcham Kharmokyong.............................62

7. Tagzigza Manggye Salgyema.........................64

8. Urgyenza Rigngen Düdtsikyong....................66

9. Gyagar Phamthingza Thuchenma................68

10. Gyaza Salwa Wödron.................................70

11. Yorpoza Drime Dangdenma.........................72

12. Chöza Wökyi Dzutrultön............................74

13. Drushaza Dzutrul Natsogtön.......................76

14. Lunggyenza Nangwa Datönma.....................78

15. Menyagza Thogbebma................................80

16. Urgyenza Namkhacham...............................82

17. Shiwerza Wöthangma.................................84

18. Khacheza Gyendenma..................................86

19. Gyerza Dragchentsal..................................88

20. Namkha Nyima Wödenma..........................90

21. Nyima Tongkhyabma..................................92

22. Khandro Mahasukasidtima..........................94

23. Chöza Bönmo..96

24..98

25..98

26..98

27..99

28..100

29..101

30..102

སྤྱི་རྒྱུད་ཆེན་མོ་ནམ་མཁའ་དཀར་པོ་ཡེ་ཁྲི་མཐའ་སེལ་ལས་ཕོ་བརྒྱུད་དང་མོ་བརྒྱུད་གཉིས་ཀྱི་དོན་གྱི་གདམས་སྐོར་ལས་མོ་བརྒྱུད་བརྡ་དོན་སུམ་ཅུ་པ་བཞུགས་སོ།།............................104

THIRTY SIGNS AND MEANINGS OF THE FEMALE LINEAGE from The Cycle of Essential Instructions of the Male and Female Lineages, from The Great General Tantra, White Sky: Liberating Extremes of the Mind..105

མཁའ་འགྲོ་ཆོ་ཟ་བོན་མོའི་གསོལ་འདེབས།..132

PRAYER TO KHANDRO CHÖZA BÖNMO..132

THE LAMP OF THE FORTUNATE MIND: A hagiography of Khandro Chöza Bönmo...135

Her birth..138

Meeting her Root Master..139

How she practised great, unsurpassable Dzogchen.......141

The great deeds Chöza performed for the doctrines and the benefit of all sentient beings.................................148

Chöza Bönmo's subsequent emanations for the benefit of sentient beings..153

How she manifested the final integration with the Natural State..154

མཁའ་འགྲོ་ཅོ་ཟ་བོན་མོའི་རྣམ་ཐར་སྐལ་ལྡན་སེམས་ཀྱི་སྒྲོན་མེ།། 157

སྐུ་སྐྱེ་བ་བཞེས་པའི་སྐོར།..159

བཤེས་གཉེན་གྱི་བླ་མ་དམ་པ་རྣམས་དང་མཇལ་ཚུལ།..................................160

བླ་མེད་རྫོགས་པ་ཆེན་པོའི་དོན་ལ་ཉམས་ལེན་གནང་ཚུལ།..............................161

བསྟན་འགྲོའི་དོན་ཆེན་མཛད་པའི་སྐོར།..164

གདུལ་བྱ་གཞན་དོན་དུ་སྤྲུལ་སྐུ་བྱོན་ཚུལ།..167

ཐ་མ་དབྱིངས་སུ་གཤེགས་ཚུལ།...168

མཁའ་འགྲོ་ཅོ་ཟ་བོན་མོའི་གསོལ་འདེབས། 169

Prayer to Lachen Drenpa Namkha..171

བླ་ཆེན་དྲན་པ་ནམ་མཁའི་གསོལ་འདེབས་བཞུགས་སོ།། 171

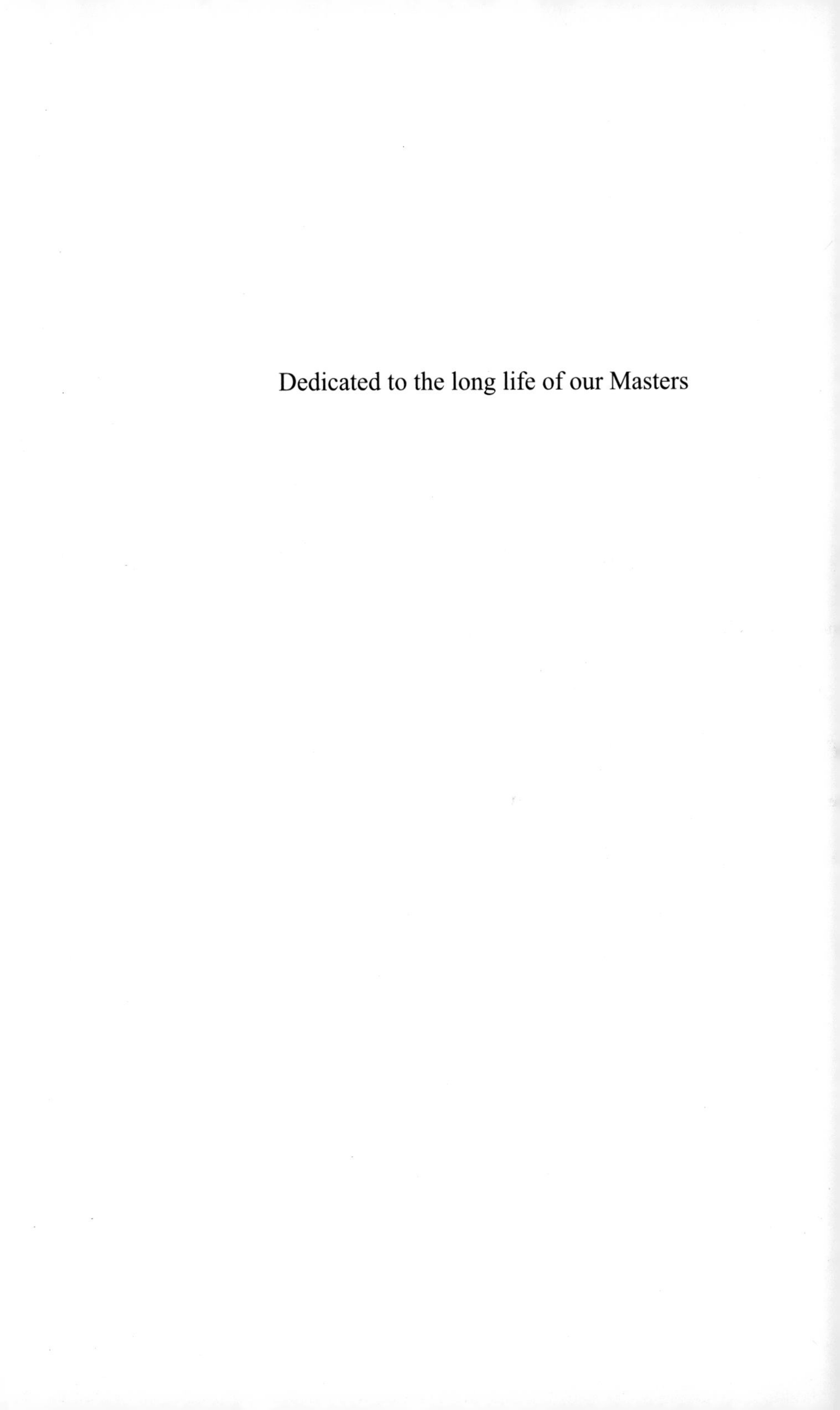

Dedicated to the long life of our Masters

FOREWORD

by

Yongdzin Lopön Tenzin Namdak Rinpoche

རྫོགས་པ་ཆེན་པོ་ཡེ་ཁྲི་མཐའ་སེལ་གྱི་བརྒྱུད་པའི་བླ་མ་མོ་བརྒྱུད་ཀྱི་གདམས་པ་
དང་སྐུ་བརྙན་གྱི་ཟུང་འཇུག་འདི་པར་བསྐྲུན་བྱས་པའི་དགེ་བས་བསྟན་འགྲོར་ཕན་
བདེ་འབྱུང་བའི་རྒྱུ་གྱུར་ཅིག།

བསྟན་འཛིན་རྣམ་དག་བྲིས།

May the merits of publishing both the images and the instructions of the female lineage holders from the lineage masters of *Dzogpa Chenpo Yetri Thasel* bring benefit to both the doctrines and sentient beings!

Written by Tennam

14 August, 2010, Shenten Dargye Ling

PREFACE

Yongdzin Lopön Tenzin Namdak Rinpoche has kindly taught the *Thirty Signs and Meanings of the Female Lineage*, the Mogyud,[1] from the *Cycle of Essential Instructions of the Male and Female Lineages* of the *Yetri Thasel*[2] Dzogchen cycle to his western students on two occasions, firstly in Paris, 1999, and more recently, in Pfauenhof, Germany, in 2009. Although Dmitry and I were not able to attend the second retreat, the Yungdrung Bön Stiftung commissioned us to make a transcript using audio and video recordings. We were surprised to discover that there were no *tsakali* images of the Khandro. When we asked Yongdzin Rinpoche about this, he replied that not only were there no *tsakali*, but that indeed *thangkas* of the Mogyud cycle are extremely rare. However, he went on to say that the descriptions and attributes of each woman lineage holder were clearly detailed in the text, and that, if people were interested, a *thangka* could be executed. Everyone was of course very excited by this project, a sponsor was found, and Yongdzin Rinpoche himself set about drawing up a blueprint for the new *thangka*, which was to be painted by Pönzang Geshe Mönlam Wangyal in Triten Norbutse Bönpo Monastery, Kathmandu, Nepal. You will notice several differences between the *thangka* itself and the text compiled by Yongdzin Rinpoche; the painter had recourse to other texts and did not follow this one precisely.

Once the *thangka* and transcript were ready, Yongdzin Rinpoche instructed us to combine the two in a book for practitioners. Nagru Geshe Gelek Jinpa was also very enthusiastic about this project and felt it would be of great benefit to translate the root text so that those who have received Yongdzin Rinpoche's precious and perfect teachings would have the chance to read the Tibetan text, too. It is not within the scope of this project to translate the whole of the Dzogchen *Yetri Thasel Mogyud*, so we decided to concentrate on the heart advice of the Khandro which Yongdzin Rinpoche had already taught.

[1] Tib. mo brgyud.

[2] Tib. *sPyi rgyud chen po nam mkha' dkar po ye khri mtha 'sel las pho brgyud dang mo brgyud gnyis kyi don gyi gdams skor las mo brgyud brda don sum cu pa bzhugs so.*

Yetri Thasel is one of the major cycles of Bönpo Dzogchen and as a whole, a Nyengyud,[3] an Oral Tradition, which Lungbön Lhanyen[4] received from the sage Tsewang Rigdzin.[5] Although this book mainly focuses on the teachings of the Mogyud lineage of *Yetri Thasel*, Yongdzin Rinpoche has also taught the general summary of the Dzogchen View from the Phogyud,[6] the male lineage. The transmission of this lineage extends from Bönku Kuntu Zangpo up to the present lineage holder, Yongdzin Rinpoche himself. A general outline of the succession of masters is as follows:

Bönku Kuntu Zangpo[7]
Nangsrid Kunsal Wöjye Gyalpo[8]
Sanggag Kunchang Gyalpo[9]
Katog Donthong Gyalpo[10]

Yeshe Wökyi Lama[11]
Kunsal Wökyi Khyeu[12]

Three brothers:
Kheu Dagpa[13]
Kheu Salwa[14]
Kheu Shepa.[15]

After many generations the lineage came to Zhang Zhung Gakhyung Pungpa,[16] and from him it passed into India to:
Sewö Yungdrung Drubpa.[17]

---

[3] Tib. snyan rgyud.
[4] Tib. Lung bon Lha gnyan, b. 1088.
[5] Tib. Tshe dbang Rig 'dzin.
[6] Tib. pho gyud.
[7] Tib. Kun tu bZang po.
[8] Tib. sNang srid Kun gsal 'Od 'byed rGyal po.
[9] Tib. gSang sngags Kun 'chang rGyal po.
[10] Tib. bKa' rtogs Don mthong rGyal po.
[11] Tib. Ye shes 'Od kyi Bla ma.
[12] Tib. Kun gsal 'Od kyi Khyeu.
[13] Tib. Khe'u Dag pa alias Tib. sTon pa gTo rgyal Ye mkhyen - Buddha of the previous Yungdrung Bön cycle.
[14] Tib. Khe'u gSal ba alias Tib. sTon pa gShen rab Mi bo che - Buddha of the current Yungdrung Bön cycle.
[15] Tib. Khe'u Shes pa alias Tib. sTon pa Thang ma Me sgron - Buddha of the next Yungdrung Bön cycle.
[16] Tib. Zhang zhung Ga khyung sPungs pa - reincarnation of dMu ra Ta han (sTon pa gShen rab Mi bo).
[17] Tib. gSas 'od g.Yung drung Grub pa.

Many generations later it reached:
Shen Maksha Setsa[18]
Drenpa Namkha[19]
Tsewang Rigdzin[20]
Lungbön Lhanyen (b.1088)
Lungbön Khorlo Gyalpo.

After many generations, it came to Yongdzin Lopön Tenzin Namdak Rinpoche.

One of the principle holders of this Mogyud lineage was Chöza Bönmo, an amazing woman who lived in Tibet in the eighth century and played a vital role in preserving Yungdrung Bön during this time of severe persecution. As an inspiration to western students, Geshe Gelek kindly took it upon himself to compose a short biography of this extraordinary lady, who ultimately achieved the rainbow body of the great transfer. Although there are many stories about the miraculous feats of this great yogini, Geshe Gelek chose to base his account on the teaching texts. In doing so, he clearly illustrates how Chöza Bönmo received Dzogchen teachings and what she practised in order to fully realize the Nature of her own Mind. This is truly a rare and precious gift for western students, as although our Masters have kindly told us many inspiring stories from the lives of the great lineage holders of the *Zhang Zhung Nyengyud*[21] teachings, there are only scant records of precisely what these ancient masters practised. Here, however, we learn not only what Chöza Bönmo practised, but also the sequence in which she practised, and the fruit of each stage of her practice. This is a path we can all aspire to follow.

As Yongdzin Rinpoche said when he taught these teachings:

"These Khandro didn't just descend from some heaven. They were human beings who practised, achieved realisation, and finally taught their student. [...] All these Dakinis came from different nationalities

[18] Tib. gShen Ma ksha Se tsa.
[19] Tib. Dran pa Nam mkha'.
[20] Tib. Tshe dbang rig 'dzin.
[21] Tib. *Zhang zhung snyan rgyud* - the most important Bönpo Dzogchen cycle. See Namdak, Yongdzin Lopön Tenzin, transc. & ed. Ermakova, C. & Ermakov, D. *Masters of the Zhang Zhung Nyengyud: Pith Instructions from the Experiential Transmission of Bönpo Dzogchen*, (New Delhi: Heritage Publishers, 2010).

but there are no Westerners among them, unfortunately. So then try, ladies, at least one or two!"

It is our sincere hope and wish that this book will be of benefit to all sentient beings.

Shenten Dargye Ling, fifteenth day of first month of the Iron Rabbit year, 19 March, 2011.

ACKNOWLEDGEMENTS

Producing a book, particularly one as important as a teaching text, is a serious and time consuming undertaking, and this publication would not have been possible without the generous support of many friends and *sangha* members.

First of all we would like to express our heartfelt gratitude to Yongdzin Rinpoche for his precious teachings, his readiness to oversee the painting of the *thangka*, his patience in clarifying our questions, and also for his personal encouragement and enthusiasm for this project. We would also like to thank Khenpo Tenpa Yungdrung for his support, Geshe Samten Tsukphü for verifying the Tibetan orthography, and Geshe Gelek Jinpa for holding western practitioners in his heart as he compiled Chöza Bönmo's biography, and for his energetic, inspiring translation of the root text.

We are also grateful to Richard Williamson for his help in editing the images of the Khandro and for bringing the prints from Kathmandu.

Thanks also go to Graham Hill, Jane Weston and Mariette Wiebenga for proofreading, and Jamie Hamilton for help in acquiring the necessary software.

And finally, we would like to thank all those who supported this project financially: Marie-Jose Arnautin, Melanie Boss, Martin Bugter, Michael Canter, Jean Cavaillès, Sophie Frisch, Margit Groener, Andreas Gruetzmacher, Renato Gucci, Norbert Halder, Dieter Hoberg, Dr. Janos Kazsoki, Andrea Klug, Gideon Makin, Claire Mosser, Dr. Jens Rowold, Rev. Alan and Pearl Stears, Takahiko Wakishima, Yungdrung Wangmo, Ingrid Weidemann, Benno Wrobel; Sabine, Christian and Malou; the Mexican *sangha*; the Sardinian *sangha*; the Yungdrung Bön Stiftung; and other anonymous donors.

Dzogchen Yetri Thasel Mogyud Lineage

རྫོགས་ཆེན་ཡེ་ཁྲིའི་བརྒྱུད་རིམ་མཁའ་འགྲོའི་ཚོགས་ཀྱི་བཀོད་པ།

Arrangement of the *Dzogchen Yetri Thasel* Mogyud Lineage

རྫོགས་ཆེན་ཡེ་ཁྲིའི་བརྒྱུད་རིམ་མཁའ་འགྲོའི་ཚོགས་ཀྱི་བཀོད་པ།

THE KHANDRO CYCLE OF MOGYUD

Spelling, Transliteration and Translation of the names

The spelling of the names varies in the root text and in The Arrangement of the Khandro Mogyud Lineage for the Thangka. *Furthermore, Yongdzin Rinpoche sometimes used other forms of the names during his oral teaching. These variations are included in this list.*

C. ཡུམ་ས་ཏྲིག་ཨེར་སངས།

Yum Sa trig Er sangs. Yum Satrig Ersang. Great Mother, Loving Goddess of Wisdom. Bon sku (Dharmakaya) form.

1a. མཛེས་མ་ཡིད་འོང་མ།

mDzes ma Yid 'ong ma. Dzema Yiwongma. Lovely Beautiful Khandro. rDzogs sku (Sambhogakaya) form.

1b. རྒྱ་གར་མཁའ་འགྲོ་ཨུ་ལི་ཤག (ཨུ་ལི་ཤ།)

rGya gar mKha' 'gro U li shag (U li sha). Gyagarma Khandro Ulishak (Ulisha). Indian Khandro Ulishak. sPrul sku (Nirmanakaya) form.[1]

2. དབལ་མོ་ཟ་ནམ་མཁའ་འོད་ཀྱི་རྒྱལ་མོ། (དབལ་ཟ་འོད་ཀྱི་རྒྱལ་མོ།)

dBal mo za Nam mkha' 'Od kyi rGyal mo (dBal za 'Od kyi rGyal mo). Walmoza Namkha Wökyi Gyalmo (Walza Wökyi Gyalmo). Queen of the Light of the Sky of the Wal clan.

3. རྭ་ཞགས་ཟ་གསལ་བ་དབྱུངས་ཕྱུག་མ། (གསལ་བའི་དབྱིངས་ཕྱུག་མ།)

Rwa zhags za gSal ba dByings phyug ma (gSal ba'i dByings phyug ma). Razhagza Salwa Yingchyugma (Salwai Yingchyugma). Luminous Lady of Space of the Razhag clan.

4. ཞང་ཞུང་ཟ་འོད་ཀྱི་བླ་མ། (ཞང་ཞུང་མཁའ་འགྲོ་འོད་ཀྱི་བླ་མ།)

Zhang zhung za 'Od kyi Bla ma (Zhang zhung mKha' 'gro 'Od kyi Bla ma). Zhang Zhungza Wökyi Lama (Zhang Zhung Khandro

[1] Ulisha(k) is an aspect of Dzema Yiwongma so they are represented by one image on the *thankga*.

Wökyi Lama). Spiritual Mother of Light from Zhang Zhung.

5. ལྡོང་ལྕམ་མཁར་མོ་སྐྱོང་།

lDong lcam 'Khar mo skyong. Dongcham Kharmokyong. Kharmokyong[2] from the Dong clan.

6. སྟག་གཟིག་ཟ་མང་བྱེད་གསལ་བྱེད་འོད། (མང་བྱེད་གསལ་བྱེད་མ།)

sTag gzig za Mang byed gSal byed 'od (Mang byed gSal byed ma). Tagzigza Manggye Salgyewö (Manggye Salgyema). Great Illuminating Light from Tagzig

7. ཨུ་རྒྱན་ཟ་རིགས་ངན་བདུད་རྩི་སྐྱོང་། (བདུད་རྩི་སྐྱོང་།)

U rgyan za Rigs ngan bDud rtsi skyong (bDud rtsi skyong). Urgyenza Rigngen Dütsikyong (Düdtsikyong). Holder of Nectar Low-cast Lady from Urgyen.

8. རྒྱ་གར་ཕ་མཐིང་ཟ་མཐུ་ཆེན་མ། (ཕམ་མཐིང་མཐུ་ཆེན་མ།)

rGya gar Pha mthing za mThu chen ma (Pham mthing mThu chen ma). Gyagar Phamthingza Thuchenma (Phamthing Thuchenma). Great Powerful Indian Lady from the Pamthing clan.

9. རྒྱ་ཟ་གསལ་བ་འོད་སྒྲོན། (གསལ་བའི་འོད་སྒྲོན་མ།)

rGyaza gSal ba 'Od sgron (gSal ba'i 'Od sgron ma). Gyaza Salwa Wödron (Salwai Wödronma). Chinese Lady Lamp of Clear Light.

10. གཡོར་པོ་ཟ་དྲི་མེད་མདངས་ལྡན་མ། (དྲི་མེད་མདངས་ལྡན་མ།)

gYor po za Dri med mDangs ldan ma (Dri med mDangs ldan ma). Yorpoza Drime Dangdänma (Drime Dangdänma). Lady of the Yorpo clan who possesses Pure Radiance.

11. གཙོ་ཟ་འོད་ཀྱི་རྫུ་འཕྲུལ་སྟོན།

gCo za 'Od kyi rDzu 'phrul ston. Chöza Wökyi Dzutrultön. Lady from the Chö clan who shines Miraculously.

12. བྲུ་ཤ་ཟ་རྫུ་འཕྲུལ་སྣ་ཚོགས་སྟོན། (རྫུ་འཕྲུལ་སྣ་ཚོགས་སྟོན།)

Bru sha za rDzu 'phrul sNa tshogs ston (rDzu 'phrul sNa tshogs ston). Drushaza Dzutrul Natsogtön (Dzutrul Natsogtön). Lady from Drusha who shows many Miracles.

[2] Both Geshe Gelek Jinpa and Yongdzin Rinpoche commented that this name cannot be translated as it is not in the Tibetan language.

13. ལུང་རྒྱན་ཟ་སྣང་བ་བརྡ་སྟོན་མ། (ལུང་རྒྱན་སྣང་བ་བརྡ་སྟོན་མ།)

Lung rgyan za sNang ba brDa ston ma (Lung rgyan sNang ba brDa ston ma). Lunggyenza Nangwa Datönma (Lunggyen Nangwa Datönma). Lady from Lunggyen who shows the Signs of Visions.

14. མེ་ཉག་ཟ་ཐོག་འབེབས་མ། (མེ་ཉག་ཐོག་འབེབ་འོད་ཟེར་མ།)

Me nyag za Thog 'bebs ma (Me nyag Thog 'bebs 'Od zer ma). Menyagza Thogbebma (Menyag Thogbeb Wözerma). (Light Rays) from Menyag who entered Direct Understanding.

15. ཨུ་རྒྱན་ཟ་ནམ་མཁའ་ལྕམ། (གནམ་ལྕགས་འོད་འཕྲོ་མ།)

U rgyan za Nam mkha' lcam (gNam lcags 'Od 'phro ma). Urgyenza Namkhacham (Namchag Wötroma). Lady of Space from Urgyen (Light Radiating Thunderbolt Lady).

16. ཤི་བེར་ (ཤེལ་ཝེར་) ཟ་འོད་ཐང་མ།

Shi ber (Shel wer) za 'Od thang ma. Shiwerza (Shelwerza) Wöthangma. Light of Serenity from the Shiver (Shelwer) clan.

17. ཁ་ཆེ་ཟ་རྒྱན་ལྡན་མ། (རྒྱན་ལྡན་མ།)

Kha che za rGyan ldan ma (rGyan ldan ma). Khacheza Gyendenma (Gyendenma). Ornamented Lady from Kashmir.

18. གྱེར་ཟ་ (ཟླ་) བྲག་ཆེན་རྩལ།

Gyer za (zla) Brag chen rtsal. Gyerza (Gyerda) Dragchentsal. Bön Lady who is like a Mighty Rock.

19. ནམ་མཁའ་ཉི་མ་འོད་ལྡན་མ། (མཁའ་འགྲོ་ཉི་མ་འོད་ལྡན་མ།)

Nam mkha' Nyi ma 'Od ldan ma (mKha' 'gro Nyi ma 'Od ldan ma). Namkha Nyima Wödenma (Khandro Nyima Wödenma). Glorious Sun shining in Space (Glorious Sun Khandro).

20. མཁའ་འགྲོ་ཉི་མ་སྟོང་ཁྱབ་མ། (ཉི་མ་སྟོང་ཁྱབ།)

mKha' 'gro Nyi ma sTong khyab ma (Nyi ma sTong khyab). Khandro Nyima Tongkhyabma (Nyima Tongkhyab). Lady who Shines like a Thousand all-encompassing Suns.

21. མཁའ་འགྲོ་མ་ཧ་སུ་ཀ་སིད་ཏི་ (སི་ཏི་མ།)

mKha' 'gro Ma ha su ka Sid ti (Si ti ma). Khandro Mahasukasidti (Mahasukasitima). Lady who accomplished Great Bliss.

22. མཁའ་འགྲོ་ཅོ་ཟ་བོན་གཅིག་༼མ།༽ ༼ཅོ་ཟ་བོན་མོ།༽

mKha' 'gro Co za Bon gcig (ma) (Co za Bon mo). Khandro Chöza Bönchig(ma) (Chöza Bönmo). Sole Mother of the Doctrines Khandro of the Chö clan.

THE ARRANGEMENT OF THE KHANDRO MOGYUD LINEAGE FOR THE THANGKA

by Yongdzin Lopön Tenzin Namdak Rinpoche

This arrangement of the hosts of Khandro from the Dzogchen Yetri Thasel *transmission lineage is according to the* Yetri Thasel Mogyud Chapter, *and also from the propitiation text for the Mogyud lineage of* Tsewang Gyagarma *as well as from the secret* Practice of Drenpa Namkha *and also the* Practice Cycle of Lishu Tagring.

I take refuge in and prostrate to the hosts of Khandro of the three dimensions!

According to these texts it is the Great Mother Satrig Ersang who is the source of the manifestation of the Khandro.[1] She is the chief deity in the centre. She has one face, two hands, and is seated cross-legged on a lion throne topped with cushions of a sun, moon and lotus.

Her two hands are in the anticlockwise *mudra* of a lotus, each holding the stem of a flower. On the lotus flower on her right are the five heroic syllables. The lotus flower on her left is ornamented with the clear mirror of existence. Her body is yellow in colour, and she is adorned with the thirteen peaceful ornaments.[2]

---

[1] In this text Satrig Ersang is not numbered but in the *thangka* she appears as the central figure.

[2] Tib. long sku'i rgyan chas bcu gsum: 1. dbu rgyan - crown; 2. snyan cha - (two) earrings; 3. mgul chu - choker; 4. do sham - long necklace; 5. se mo do - middle necklace; 6. dpung rgyan - (two) armlets; 7. phyag gdub - (two) bracelets; 8. zhabs gdub - (two) anklets; 9. gdan khri - throne; 10. stod yogs - upper cloth; 11. smad sham - lower garment; 12. rgyab yol - back- and head rest; 13. dbu gdugs - umbrella.

1. Gyagar Dzema Yiwongma Ulisha.[3]

She has one face, two hands, and is standing in the dancing posture with her left leg bent and her right leg outstretched. Her body is blue in colour. She is adorned with precious ornaments and the six bone ornaments.[4] She is wearing garments of fine silk and satin. She is standing on cushions of a lotus, sun and moon. She is looking at a river in front of her, and her actions show the sign of achievement.[5]

2. Walza Wökyi Gyalmo.

She has one face, two hands and her body is yellow in colour. She appears like a Khandro standing in space. She is fully adorned with precious jewels and the six bone ornaments. She is dispatching groups of peaceful and wrathful divinities from her heart.

3. Salwai Yingchyugma.

She has one face, two hands, and her body is red in colour. She is wearing an upper garment and a skirt. She is adorned with many precious ornaments. She is sitting cross-legged on lotus and sun cushions. She shows the action of clearly brandishing a *phurpa*[6] in space.

4. Zhang Zhung Khandro Wökyi Lama.

She has one face, two hands, and her body is pink in colour. She is radiantly beautiful. She is wearing a vest and skirt of fine silk and satin. She is adorned with precious jewellery. She is seated on sun and moon cushions with one leg bent, the other outstretched. She

---

[3] Yongdzin Rinpoche explained that since Ulisha is an aspect of Dzema Yiwongma, they are represented by one image on the *thangka*. Spellings of the Khandro names also differ, depending on the text. Here it is spelled Tib. U li sha. An alternative spelling is Tib. U li shag. For spellings in Tibetan and Wylie system as well as the names' translation see The Khandro Cycle of Mogyud, p. 19.

[4] Tib. rus pa'i rgyan drug: 1. dbu rgyan dang de'i 'khor lo - crown ornament; 2. snyan cha a lung gnyis - (two) earrings; 3. mgul rgyan phreng ba - necklace; 4. phyag zhabs kyi gdub bu - (two) hand and (two) ankle bracelets; 5. lus rgyan pa tra - body ornaments; 6. ku rgyan ska rags - sash ornaments.

[5] Rinpoche explains: she is watching or looking into water, and sometimes she makes magical signs on the water.

[6] Tib. pur pa - tantric dagger.

spins wheels of light in space.

5. Dongcham Kharmokyong.

She has one face, two hands, and her body is yellow in colour. She is naked, adorned with the six bone ornaments and clad in a single, flowing garment of pure satin. She is riding on the sun.

6. Manggye Salgyema.

She has one face, two hands, and her body is maroon in colour. She is standing in the dancing posture, naked and adorned with bone ornaments. Rainbow lights and rays of the five colours appear from her body. She is brandishing a *phurpa* in space.

7. Düdtsikyong.

She has one face, two hands, and her body is blue in colour. She is covered in beautiful leaves. Her left leg is half bent, her right leg is stretched. She is seated on sun and moon cushions. She causes myriads of precious jewels as well as nuggets of gold and turquoise to fall like rain.

8. Phamting Thuchenma.

She has one face, two hands, and her body is dark blue in colour. Her appearance is like that of a Khandro. She is naked, adorned with bone ornaments. She is showing the sign of teaching Bön and riding a turquoise-coloured dragon in the sky.

9. Salwai Wödronma.

She has one face, two hands, and her body is pale yellow in colour. She is dressed in fine silk and satin. Her body is gleaming. She looks heroic and is riding a lion.

10. Drime Dangdenma.

She has one face, two hands, and her body is a glowing brown in colour. She is dressed in silk and cotton, and adorned with precious ornaments. She is wearing an upper garment and a skirt. Various ornaments decorate her head and many bracelets adorn her arms. She is showing the action of striding through space.

11. Chöza Wökyi Dzutrultön.

She has one face, two hands, and her body is white with a radiant red hue. She has the appearance of a Khandro. She is clad completely in silk and adorned with all the bone ornaments. She extracts the essence of the elements and is stepping on a lake.

12. Dzutrul Natsogtön.

She has one face, and two hands. She is half-sitting on a lotus and sun disc with one leg drawn up, the other half bent. Many flowers adorn her whole body. She is sending tigers and leopards to do her bidding.

13. Lunggyen Nangwa Datönma.

She has one face, two hands, and her body is maroon in colour. She is standing in the pose of a Khandro dancing. She is adorned with precious jewels and bone ornaments. She is wearing garments of fine silk and satin. A rain of life-giving nectar cascades from her body. She is holding a pouch of auspiciousness, showing the action of saving sentient beings' lives and performing generosity.

14. Menyag Thogbeb Wözerma.

She has one face, two hands, and her body is red in colour. She is in the pose of a dancing Khandro. Adorned with the six ornaments, she is standing in the midst of a blazing fire.

15. Namchag Wötroma.

She has one face, two hands, and her body is yellow in colour. She is standing in the pose of a Khandro dancing, adorned with bone ornaments. A rain of nectar cascades unceasingly from her body. From her hands she generously bestows medicinal nectar.

16. Shelwer Wötroma.

She has one face, two hands, and her body is dark blue in colour. She is standing in the pose of a Khandro dancing, adorned with bone ornaments and clad in garments of fine silk and satin. Her body possesses majestic power, so she naturally suppresses obstacles, provocations, bad spirits, and flesh-eating ghouls.

17. Gyendenma.

She has one face, two hands, and her body is maroon in colour. She has the appearance of a dancing Khandro. She is wearing bone ornaments and skull beads. Her garments are made of satin and fine silk. She sends many emanations from her body and shows the action of draping her clothes over sunbeams.

18. Gyerda Dragchentsal.

She has one face, two hands, and the appearance of a Khandro. She is adorned with the usual ornaments of a Khandro, and skull beads. She is clad in garments of silk and satin, and her body is yellowy-green in colour. She displays the miracle of swift-footedness.

19. Khandro Nyima Wödenma.

She has one face, two hands, and her body is red in colour. Naked, she is adorned with the six bone ornaments, and clad in a single garment of flowing silk and satin. Her hair is loose. In her right hand she holds a drum and *shang*,[7] in her left hand she holds a *thodpa*.[8] Rays of light emanate from her body. She is showing the action of striding through space.

20. Khandro Nyima Tongkhyabma.

She has one face, two hands, and her body is white in colour. She is standing and dancing. She is adorned with bone ornaments, and in her left hand she holds a *thodpa*. She is showing the action of tethering the sun and moon.

21. Khandro Mahasukasitima.

She has one face, two hands, and her body is white in colour. Her clothes are made of fine silk and satin. She is seated in the position of equipoise, emanating many lights from her body.

22. Khandro Chöza Bönchigma.

She has one face, two hands, and the appearance of a Khandro. Her body is white in colour. She is decorated with cemetery ornaments. She holds a *khatwam*[9] trident in her right hand and a skull in her

[7] Tib. gshang - Bönpo flat bell.
[8] Tib. thod pa - skull cap.
[9] Tib. kha twam ga - tantric staff with skulls piled one above another at

left hand. She is standing in the centre of myriads of rainbows and lights which manifest from her body.

Translated by Nagru Geshe Gelek Jinpa, Carol Ermakova and Dmitry Ermakov, Shenten Dargye Ling, Blou, France, March 2011.

---

the top, often topped with a trident.

༄།། རྫོགས་ཆེན་ཡེ་ཁྲིའི་བརྒྱུད་རིམ་མཁའ་འགྲོའི་ཚོགས་ཀྱི་བཀོད་པ་ཡེ་ཁྲིའི་མཁའ་འགྲོ་མོ་བརྒྱད་ཀྱི་ལེའུ་དང་། ཚེ་དབང་རྒྱ་གར་མའི་མོ་བརྒྱད་ཀྱི་སྒྲུབ་ཐབས་དང་། དྲན་པ་གསང་སྒྲུབ། ལི་ཤུའི་སྒྲུབ་སྐོར་རྣམས་དང་བསྟུན་ནས། མཁའ་འགྲོ་མོ་བརྒྱད་ཀྱི་ཞལ་ཐང་གི་བཀོད་པ་ནི།

༈ གནས་གསུམ་མཁའ་འགྲོའི་ཚོགས་ལ་ཕྱག་འཚལ་ཞིང་སྐྱབས་སུ་མཆིའོ།། སྐབས་འདིའི་མཁའ་འགྲོའི་སྤྱིལ་གཞི་ཡུམ་ཆེན་མོ་ས་ཏྲིག་ཨེར་སངས་ཡིན་པར་གསུངས་པས། གཙོ་མོ་ས་ཏྲིག་ཨེར་སངས་ཞལ་གཅིག་ཕྱག་གཉིས། ཞབས་སྐྱིལ་དཀྱུང་སེང་ཁྲི་ཉི་ཟླ་པད་མའི་གདན་ལ་བཞུགས་པ། ཕྱག་གཉིས་ཐུགས་ཁར་པད་སྐོར་གཡས་སུ་འཁྱིལ་ཞིང་པད་སྡོང་གི་ཡུ་བ་ནས་འཛིན་པ། པད་སྡོང་གཡས་ཀྱི་སྟེང་དུ་ཡིག་གེ་དཔའ་འོ་འབྲུ་ལྔ། གཡོན་གྱི་པད་སྡོང་ཁར་སྣང་གསལ་གྱི་མེ་ལོང་བརྒྱན་པ།སྐུ་མདོག་སེར་མོ། ཞི་བའི་རྒྱན་བཅུ་གསུམ་གྱིས་བརྒྱན་པ།

༡༽ རྒྱ་གར་མཁའ་འགྲོ་མཛེས་མ་ཡིད་འོང་མའམ་ཨུ་ལི་ཤ། ཞལ་གཅིག་ཕྱག་གཉིས་གར་སྟབས། ཞབས་གཡས་བསྐུམ། གཡོན་བརྐྱང་། སྐུ་མདོག་སྔོན་མོ། རིན་པོ་ཆེ་དང་རུས་པའི་རྒྱན་དྲུག་གིས་བརྒྱན་པ། དར་ཟབ་ཀྱི་ན་བ་བཟའ་གསོལ་ཞིང་། པད་ཉི་ཟླ་བའི་གདན་ལ་བཞེངས་པ། མདུན་དུ་ཆུ་བོའི་སྟེང་དུ་གཟིགས་ཤིང་གྲུབ་རྟགས་འཛོག་པའི་ཚུལ་ཅན།

༢༽ དབལ་ཟ་འོད་ཀྱི་རྒྱལ་མོ། ཞལ་གཅིག་ཕྱག་གཉིས། སྐུ་མདོག་སེར་མོ། མཁའ་འགྲོའི་ཆ་ལུགས་གར་སྟབས་ཅན་བར་སྣང་དུ་བཞེངས་པ། རིན་པོ་ཆེ་དང་རུས་པའི་རྒྱན་དྲུག་གིས་སྤྲས་པ། ཐུགས་ཁ་ནས་ཞི་ཁྲོའི་ལྷ་ཚོགས་འཕྲོད་པ།

༣༽ གསལ་བའི་དབྱིངས་ཕྱུག་མ། ཞལ་གཅིག་ཕྱག་གཉིས། སྐུ་མདོག་དམར་མོ། སྟོད་གཡོག་དང་སྨད་ཤམ། རིན་ཆེན་གྱི་རྒྱན་ཆ་ཅན། པད་ཉིའི་སྟེང་དུ་ཞབས་སྐྱིལ་ཀྲུང་གིས་བཞུགས་ཤིང་། བར་སྣང་དུ་ཕུར་པ་འཛུག་པའི་ཚུལ་ཅན།

༤༽ ཞང་ཞུང་མཁའ་འགྲོ་འོད་ཀྱི་བླ་མ། ཞལ་གཅིག་ཕྱག་གཉིས་སྐུ་མདོག་དཀར་དམར་མཛེས་མདངས་ཅན། དར་ཟབ་སྟོད་གཡོག་སྨད་ཤམ་རིན་ཆེན་གྱི་རྒྱན་དང་ལྡན་པ། པད་ཉི་ཟླ་བའི་གདན་ལ་ཞབས་ཕྱེད་སྐྱིལ་དུ་བཞུགས་ཤིང་བར་སྣང་དུ་འོད་ཀྱི་འཁོར་ལོ་བསྐོར་བའི་ཚུལ་ཅན།

༥༽ ལྡོང་ལྕམ་འཁོར་མོ་སྐྱོང་། ཞལ་གཅིག་ཕྱག་གཉིས་སེར་མོ། གཅེར་བུ་རུས་པའི་

རྒྱན་དྲུག་དར་དཔྱང་ཅན། ཉི་མ་ལ་ཞོན་པ།

༦༽ མང་བྱེད་གསལ་བྱེད་མ། ཞལ་གཅིག་ཕྱག་གཉིས་སྐུ་མདོག་དམར་སྨུག་གར་སྟབས་ཀྱིས་བཞེངས་པ། གཅེར་བུ་རུས་པའི་རྒྱན་ལྡན། སྐུ་ལས་གཞའ་ཚོན་སྣ་ལྔའི་འོད་ཟེར་འཕྲོ་བ། ཕུར་པ་བར་སྣང་མཁའ་ལ་འཛུག་པ།

༧༽ བདུད་རྩི་སྐྱོང་། ཞལ་གཅིག་ཕྱག་གཉིས། སྐུ་མདོག་སྔོན་མོ། སྐུ་ལ་ཤིང་ལོ་མཛེས་པ་སྣ་ཚོགས་ཀྱིས་བརྒྱན་ཞིང་ཞབས་ཕྱེད་སྐྱིལ། གཡས་བརྐྱང་། གཡོན་བསྐུམ། ཉི་ཟླའི་གདན་ལ་བཞུགས་ཤིང་རིན་པོ་ཆེ་གསེར་གཡུ་ལས་སོགས་ཀྱི་ཆར་འབེབ་པར་མཛད་པ།

༨༽ ཕམ་མཐིང་མཐུ་ཆེན་མ། ཞལ་གཅིག་ཕྱག་གཉིས། སྐུ་མདོག་མཐིང་ནག མཁའ་འགྲོའི་ཆས། གཅེར་བུ་རུས་རྒྱན་ཅན། བར་སྣང་དུ་པོན་གསུང་ཞིང་། གཡུ་འབྲུག་ཧ་རུ་ཞོན་པ།

༩༽ གསལ་བའི་འོད་སྒྲོན་མ། ཞལ་གཅིག་ཕྱག་གཉིས། སྐུ་མདོག་དཀར་སེར། དར་ཟབ་ཀྱི་ན་བ་བཟའ་གསོལ་ཞིང་སྐུ་ཤ་རྒྱས་པ། དཔའ་བོའི་གྱད་རྩལ་ཅན། སེང་གེ་ལ་བཅིབས་པ།

༡༠༽ དྲི་མེད་མདངས་ལྡན་མ། ཞལ་གཅིག་ཕྱག་གཉིས། སྐུ་མདོག་སྨུག་མདངས། དར་ཟབ་རིན་ཆེན་རྒྱན་གྱིས་བརྒྱན་པ། སྟོད་གཡོག སྨད་ཤམ། དབུ་རྒྱན་ཕྱག་གདུབ་སོགས། བར་སྣང་ཁམས་སུ་གཤེགས་ཚུལ་ཅན།

༡༡༽ གཙོ་ཟ་འོད་ཀྱི་རྫུ་འཕྲུལ་སྟོན། ཞལ་གཅིག་ཕྱག་གཉིས། སྐུ་མདོག་དཀར་ལ་དམར་བའི་མདངས། མཁའ་འགྲོའི་ཆས་ཅན་དར་དང་རུས་པའི་རྒྱན་རྫོགས། འབྱུང་བའི་བཅུད་ལེན་ཞིང་མཚོ་ཡི་སྟེང་དུ་གོམ་པས་བགྲོད་དེ་གཤེགས་པའི་ཚུལ་ཅན།

༡༢༽ རྫུ་འཕྲུལ་སྣ་ཚོགས་སྟོན། ཞལ་གཅིག་ཕྱག་གཉིས། ཞབས་ཕྱེད་སྐྱིལ་པད་ཉིའི་གདན་ལ་བཞུགས་པ། སྐུ་ལ་མེ་ཏོག་སྣ་ཚོགས་ཀྱིས་བརྒྱན་ཞིང་སྟག་དང་གཟིག་ཕོ་ཉར་འཁྱིད་པའོ།།

༡༣༽ ལུང་རྒྱན་སྣང་བ་བཟ་སྟོན་མ། ཞལ་གཅིག་ཕྱག་གཉིས། སྐུ་མདོག་དམར་སྨུག མཁའ་མགྲོའི་གར་སྟབས་ཅན། རིན་ཆེན་རུས་པའི་རྒྱན་དང་། དར་ཟབ་ཀྱི་ན་བ་

བཟའ་གསོལ་བ། སྐུ་ལས་བདུད་རྩིའི་ཆར་རྒྱུན་བབས་པས་སེམས་ཅན་གསོ་བ། ཕྱག་ན་རྟེན་འབྲེལ་གྱི་རྒྱལ་པ་བསྣམས་པས་འགྲོ་བ་གསོ་སྦྱིན་མཛད་པ།

༡༤༽ མི་ཉག་ཐོག་འབེབ་འོད་ཟེར་མ། ཞལ་གཅིག་ཕྱག་གཉིས། སྐུ་མདོག་དམར། མཁའ་འགྲོའི་ཆས་རྒྱན་གར་སྟབས་ཐུས་པའི་རྒྱན་དྲུག མེ་དཔུང་འབར་བའི་དཀྱིལ་ན་བཞེངས་པ།

༡༥༽ གནམ་ལྕགས་འོད་འཕྲོ་མ། ཞལ་གཅིག་ཕྱག་གཉིས། སྐུ་མདོག་སེར། མཁའ་འགྲོའི་ཆས་ཅན་གར་སྟབས་ཐུས་པའི་རྒྱན་ལྡན། སྐུ་ལས་བདུད་རྩིའི་ཆར་རྒྱུན་འབེབ་ཅིང་ཕྱག་གིས་བདུད་རྩི་སྨན་གྱི་སྦྱིན་པ་འགྱེད་པ།

༡༦༽ ཤེལ་ལྷེར་འོད་ཐང་མ། ཞལ་གཅིག་ཕྱག་གཉིས། སྐུ་མདོག་མཐིང་ནག མཁའ་འགྲོའི་ཆས་ཅན་གར་སྟབས་ཐུས་རྒྱན། དར་ཟབ་ཀྱི་ན་བ་བཟའ། སྐུ་གཟི་བརྗིད་དང་ལྡན་པས་གདོན་བགེགས་འདྲེ་སྲིན་ཟིལ་གྱིས་གནོན་པ།

༡༧༽ རྒྱན་ལྡན་མ། ཞལ་གཅིག་ཕྱག་གཉིས། སྐུ་མདོག་དམར་སྨུག མཁའ་འགྲོའི་ཆས། གར་སྟབས་ཐུས་རྒྱན་ཐོད་ཕྲེང་། དར་ཟབ་ཀྱི་ན་བ་བཟའ། སྐུ་ཡི་སྤྲུལ་པ་དུ་མ་འགྱེད་ཅིང་། ན་བ་བཟའ་ཉི་མའི་ཟེར་ལ་འགེལ་བའི་ཚུལ་མཛད་པ།

༡༨༽ ཀྱེར་ཟླ་བྲག་ཆེན་རྩལ། ཞལ་གཅིག་ཕྱག་གཉིས། མཁའ་འགྲོའི་ཆས་རྒྱན། ཐོད་ཕྲེང་དར་ཟབ་ན་བ་བཟའ། སྐུ་མདོག་ལྗང་སེར། ཞབས་ལ་རྐང་མགྱོགས་རྫུ་འཕྲུལ་ལྡན་པ།

༡༩༽ མཁའ་འགྲོ་ཉི་མ་འོད་ལྡན་མ། ཞལ་གཅིག་ཕྱག་གཉིས། སྐུ་མདོག་དམར། གཅེར་བུ་ཐུས་པའི་རྒྱན་དྲུག དར་ཟབ་ཀྱི་ན་བ་བཟའ་དཔྱང་ཐུ། དབུ་སྐྲ་ཁྲོལ་བ། ཕྱག་ན་ཛ་གཤང་དང་། གཡོན་ཐོད་ཞལ། སྐུ་ལ་འོད་ཟེར་འཕྲོ་བ། བར་སྣང་དུ་གཤེགས་པའི་ཚུལ་ཅན།

༢༠༽ མཁའ་འགྲོ་ཉི་མ་སྟོང་ཁྱབ་མ། ཞལ་གཅིག་ཕྱག་གཉིས། སྐུ་མདོག་དཀར། གར་སྟབས་ཐུས་རྒྱན། གཡོན་པས་ཐོད་ཞལ་བསྣམས་པ། ཉི་མ་ཟླ་བ་བརྟོད་ལ་གནོན་པའི་ཚུལ་ཅན།

༢༡༽ མཁའ་འགྲོ་མ་ཧ་སུ་ཀ་སི་ཏི་མ། ཞལ་གཅིག་ཕྱག་གཉིས། སྐུ་མདོག་དཀར། དར་ཟབ་ནབ་བཟའ་སྐུ་མཉམ་བཞག་གི་ཚུལ་དུ་བཞུགས་ཤིང་སྐུ་ལུས་འོད་ཀྱི་ཕུང་

པོར་སྤྲུལ་པའོ། །

༢༢༽ མཁའ་འགྲོ་གཙོ་ཟླ་བོན་གཅིག་མ། ཞལ་གཅིག་ཕྱག་གཉིས། མཁའ་འགྲོའི་ཆས་ཅན། དཀར་མོ་དུང་ཁྲིད་ཏུས་པའི་རྒྱན་ཆ་ཅན། ཕྱག་གཡས་ཁ་ཏཾ། གཡོན་ཐོད་ཞལ། སྐུ་ལས་གཞན་ཚོན་འོད་ཟེར་འཕྲོ་བའི་དཀྱིལ་བཞེངས་པའོ།། །།

THE CYCLE OF ESSENTIAL DZOGCHEN INSTRUCTIONS

FROM THE MALE AND FEMALE LINEAGES OF YETRI THASEL

Teachings by Yongdzin Lopön Tenzin Namdak Rinpoche on

sPyi rgyud chen mo nam mkha' dkar po ye khri mtha' sel las pho brgyud dang mo brgyud gnyis kyi don gyi gdams skor bzhugs so

Compiled by Lachen Drenpa Namkha

given in Pfauenhof, Germany, 12th - 17th September 2009

Preliminary Comments

The origin of suffering and the way to purify it

I want to tell you the purpose of listening to the teachings. You have to think: human life is very rare. First of all, we humans must think about our common situation. We are all bound in Samsara[1] and anything in Samsara is always afflicted by miseries and sufferings. Most of the time we don't think about this; we don't realize what the sufferings and miseries of our own present time are. Although we can all feel our own sufferings – even animals can feel good or bad or have a hard time – we never think it is possible to purify these problems. That is something which we humans in particular have to think about; suffering is not the Nature – it can be purified.

How can suffering be purified? A normal being cannot fathom this as they have no experience. You may suppose you should do this or that, judge things as good or bad or have some opinion about what to do, but in fact you cannot handle the situation. If you want to know how to release your suffering, you have to follow the Buddha's teaching, The Buddha didn't just

[1] Tib. 'khor ba

order people to do things; he himself actually practised, purified his own sufferings, and achieved the final goal, so his teachings are messages about his experience, about what he did and how he achieved Buddhahood. This is what we call Buddha's teaching.

How does suffering start? How does it increase? I have to tell you this briefly as it forms the first part of the text. Every being is endowed with consciousness. There are many different types of consciousness, but in particular there is one called Kunzhi Namshe,[2] and we can say that it is like a blackboard, because whatever we do or think – whether good or bad – is kept here like a kind of trace, like a drawing on a blackboard. This trace is called a karmic cause. Usually we speak about karmic causes, about how we create them, where they are kept, how they produce results and so on. You must understand these things first and then you can think about how to purify them. If we don't talk about karmic cause, you might have some vague idea about it or think it is something slight which is easy to purify, but actually it is not easy to deal with, even though we can talk about it easily.

Kunzhi Namshe

First of all, how are karmic causes made? I have told you that the Kunzhi Namshe is like a blackboard, but we can also use the example of a store hall. In this analogy, our mental consciousness is like a very important manager who controls everything – good, bad, whatever. The other senses – the senses of our eye, ear, nose, tongue or body, the five senses – are all like servants which are controlled by this mental consciousness and have to obey all its orders. There are eight important consciousnesses and many minor ones, making fifty-one altogether. The result of whatever they do is brought back to the store hall and that is called a karmic cause, which is then kept in the Kunzhi Namshe. Ignorance – or Dagdzin[3] – is in charge and keeps these traces properly so they are never wasted while our mental consciousness – or Yidkyi Namshe[4] – is the 'owner.' Before you practise religion you must know something about how karmic cause is collected, where it is kept and how it works.

Dreams are evidence of what I have said about karmic causes being kept in the Kunzhi Namshe. When you surface from deep sleep, there is a moment before you wake up completely when your body is lying in bed but your mind or mental consciousness

[2] Tib. kun gzhi rnam shes.
[3] Tib. bdag 'dzin.
[4] Tib. yid kyi rnam shes.

has woken up and is 'walking around the store hall' so it sees the traces you have saved there. Whatever the mind sees is karmic cause. Normally, it is that karmic cause which determines the dream. Nowadays people talk about different practices or special dreams, about how to fly or transform into many different things in the dream state but that is something different and I don't know much about it. According to our texts, dreams are evidence of how karmic causes are collected and kept in the Kunzhi Namshe. Your mental consciousness wakes up and sees the karmic traces stored in the Kunzhi Namshe – that is a dream, so dreams provide evidence that the next life doesn't depend on the material body. As in a dream, your mind is still working even though your body has stopped working, so the next lifetime is only a kind of transformation as mental consciousness takes rebirth, together with karmic cause. Your mind and all your various consciousnesses and senses go on, it is only your body which rots. Everybody knows that and you can see this clearly if you go to a churchyard. But taking rebirth doesn't depend on the body. The mind is travelling from time to time, from body to body, you see, for unlimited lifetimes, just as it does in a dream. How does the mind take a new life? You have no power over this; you have to follow your own karmic cause. That is why you have no choice as to what you dream. I have heard that there are many different methods to change or control your dream but that is something different.

Four points regarding collecting karmic causes

Our various consciousnesses and perceptions are like 'collectors.' How do they collect karmic causes? There are two ways: acting and saving a cause; not acting yet saving a cause nevertheless. There are two other possibilities here: not acting and not saving a cause; acting yet not saving a cause. So there are these four points about collecting karmic cause.

1. Acting and collecting a cause

First of all, the collector or consciousness – one of the five senses for instance, such as the ocular consciousness – sees something. But this is simultaneously influenced by mental consciousness; our mental consciousness follows our ocular consciousness and judges whether what we see is good or bad, what colour it is and so on. Mental consciousness judges everything. Once the judgement regarding colour, form, smell, taste and so on has been made and everything has been collected, the trace is immediately stored in the Kunzhi Namshe. That is acting and collecting a karmic cause, the first point.

2. Not acting but collecting a cause

Even when you are relaxing in your house, peacefully and comfortably, your mind is still thinking so many different things. It is always busy. At that moment you are not acting on whatever comes to mind, but you are thinking nevertheless, and whatever you think is written down on the blackboard, or stored in the Kunzhi Namshe. Whenever you are thinking – whether your thoughts are good, bad or neutral – a trace is left, a karmic cause is created, and this is kept in the Kunzhi Namshe. That is another point: not acting yet keeping all the traces.

3. Acting but not collecting

Maybe people have heard about the early Siddhas[5] who acted in rough ways, killing people[6] and doing many other things besides but not keeping any karmic causes. Why were no traces collected? Because their actions were not influenced by mental consciousness and everything was liberated by their knowledge of the Natural State. Therefore there were no traces to be kept. They themselves purified their Kunzhi Namshe so there was no base, no store hall where things could be kept, and as a result, nothing was saved. That is the third point, acting but not collecting.

4. Neither acting nor collecting

In this case someone is not doing anything, they just abide in the Natural State.

If you are engaged in either of the first two, whether you are acting or just thinking, everything is called Samsara, karmic cause. We are trying to purify this. We are doing something like prostrations, circumambulations or reciting a hundred mantras, and all this is an attempt to purify our karmic traces. But you might think: 'Doing this doesn't go to the root of the problem, it can't purify the root at all!' No matter how many mantras you recite or how many times you prostrate, even though you are trying to purify your karmic traces, this is still quite far away from purifying the root cause. There are many methods and none of them are useless, but they don't strike the essential point, they are not able to purify the root. It is similar to cleaning a table, you see; you can wipe it once but dust will still come again and again. Sometimes you are cleaning, sometimes dust is settling again. In a similar way, sometimes you are purifying your karma, sometimes you are

[5] Tib. grub thob.

[6] This doesn't refer to ordinary killing but to Tib. grol ba - 'deliverance,' a wrathful activity used to liberate the mind-streams of wicked beings.

creating more traces.

Three ways to purify karmic causes

The focus is on cleaning these karmic causes and Buddha showed us three general methods: Sutra, Tantra and Dzogchen.[7]

For Sutra, it is Uma,[8] the Madhyamaka view, which goes directly to the point of karmic cause and tries to purify it, but still it is not sharp enough to completely remove all karmic traces. The Madhyamaka view is integrated with consciousness, and whatever is integrated with consciousness has not been completely purified. This is true even for an antidote; something still remains because the 'cleaner' itself is not clean.

The second way, Tantra, also focuses on purifying karmic causes, but here, too, something still remains because Tantric practitioners also use consciousness. There is a lot of visualization in Tantric practice and this all uses consciousness. No matter which method you use, if it is connected with consciousness, then some part of the impure things will remain.

Then finally there is the Dzogchen View, the Natural State. Here, nothing whatsoever remains integrated with consciousness, so it is completely pure – even the store hall or the Kunzhi Namshe itself liberates into Empty Nature. So there is no base; the blackboard no longer exists! When you are in the Natural State, whatever you do or whatever your senses collect is like drawing with chalk in space: there is no base.

The Suffering of Humans

Four Sufferings

The result or fruit of karmic cause is always suffering and miseries. In general, humans are afflicted by four root sufferings. These are:

- the suffering of birth;
- the suffering of death;
- the suffering of age;
- the suffering of sickness.

These are not the Nature at all; rather, all these sufferings are created by karmic cause and you have to realize they can be liberated.

Other sufferings

Rich people have another type of suffering; they have more suffering than poor people. Poor people are always thinking about

[7] Tib. mdo ngags sems gsum.

[8] Tib. dbu ma.

how to get something, even some basic necessities. They are always wanting, wanting, and that brings them more suffering. Another suffering is being afraid of running into enemies, or worrying about losing friends. This is another type of suffering. There are eight major sufferings and miseries which afflict humans in general.[9] These are not the Nature at all. Try to realize that you can actually be liberated from them, and search for an antidote: how can they be purified? You need to think about this; that is the purpose of practising religion.

When you search for a way to purify these sufferings, you will realize that Sutra, Tantra and Dzogchen are the antidotes. You should discover this yourself and choose your own path; one person cannot order another to do something. Even Buddha preached the teachings according to the personal situations of his pupils; it wouldn't have worked if he had simply given them orders. If it were possible to simply order someone then there would be no need to teach the Nine Ways of Bön.[10] In fact, all teachings are given according to the students' capacity as not everyone is able to follow everything Buddha preached; beings don't have sufficient knowledge. Therefore it is necessary to choose followers qualified for a particular path.

So first of all you should want to purify all sufferings and miseries. Then you need to know what the root of suffering is and how it grows. This is very important. Secondly, don't think that it is not possible or not true. This is something very serious. Everyone knows that death is coming, you see. You won't just disappear then. While you are alive and healthy it is all very well to say: 'I do believe this' or 'I don't believe this' – you can say many things, but when these things come – and they certainly will – you have no power at all. You always have to follow your karmic causes, but the purpose of listening to these teachings is to learn how to purify your karma and integrate the rest of your life with practice. Don't just practise in your leisure time; do something very seriously. That is my advice.

---

[9] Tib. sdug bsngal brgyad - the suffering of birth; the suffering of old age; the suffering of sickness; the suffering of death; the suffering of being separated from loved ones; the suffering of being together with despised ones; the suffering of not getting what one wants; the suffering caused by the five aggregations.

[10] Tib. theg pa rim dgu'i bon.

The summary of the View from the Male Lineage [Pho brgyud gdams pa]

The Dzogchen cycle of *Yetri Thasel* contains instructions which have been transmitted from Master to pupil in the lineage, one after the other through the ages, so the Dzogchen View has been transmitted and taught in an unbroken succession right up to now. There are two parts to the Dzogchen *Yetri Thasel*: the Male Lineage and the Female Lineage. Although generally there are a lot of female lineages, not many of them have been recorded. Here, however, both parts are included.

The Male Lineage is Phogyud Dampa.[11] However, not all the individual Siddhas of the Male Lineage are recorded and all that remains are the general instructions and the summary which teaches the *Yetri Thasel* View of Dzogchen. The second part, the Female Lineage, contains thirty teachings given by the Khandro. These short instructions sum up what each Khandro learnt and then, finally, what she experienced and taught her disciple.

So first I will teach the general summary of this Dzogchen teaching according to the Phogyud Dampa, the Male Lineage.

Three Drenpa Namkhas

If we want to practise the Dzogchen View it is very important not to simply learn it using our own knowledge, consciousness, valid cognition or perception; this is a special way. Knowledge has to come through the blessing of the Lineage Masters. We ask them, and we receive their empowerment. One of the most important Lineage Holders is Drenpa Namkha,[12] and he is of particular importance for the Dzogchen *Yetri Thasel*. Drenpa Namkha manifested three different forms in three different eras, but they all had the same name. One was born in very early times in Tagzig,[13] and his birth was kind of miraculous. Luminous lights radiated out from Dharmakaya[14] and reached a lotus, and this emanation of Drenpa Namkha formed as a human on the lotus. As those luminous lights were blue, Drenpa Namkha is usually depicted as blue in colour.

The second Drenpa Namkha was a prince of Zhang Zhung, and the third one lived in South Tibet, in the eighth century.[15]

[11] Tib. Pho brgyud gdams pa.

[12] Tib. Dran pa Nam mkha'.

[13] Tib. sTag gzigs.

[14] Tib. bon sku.

[15] For a detailed account of the three Drenpa Namkhas see Ermakov, Dmitry. *Bø and Bön: Ancient Shamanic Traditions of Siberia and Tibet in*

It was this third one who composed the *Yetri Thasel*, including the text I am teaching from now, which is a kind of summary. It is not a literary commentary but was extracted from the *Yetri Thasel*, the source for both the Female and Male Lineages. As these are both connected with Drenpa Namkha, first of all I want to teach you how to practise Guru Yoga with this Master.

Guru Yoga with Drenpa Namkha

You can look at the form of Drenpa Namkha which is blue, but don't think that he is just an image like a *thangka*[16] painting because that doesn't work, you see.

Visualize Drenpa Namkha in front of you, a little higher than your head, facing towards you. Focus on him as clearly as you can again and again. Devotion is very, very important. If your devotion is not strong, your visualization won't be very durable; even if is quite clear, it will soon disappear. Then visualize that you receive the three elements from his heart level. These look like the elements fire, water and wind but in fact they are his knowledge and wisdom which emanate from him to you and purify all your obscurations and defilements – everything is burned up, washed and blown away. After this, you become completely pure and are qualified to receive his empowerment. Then visualize that a white **A** emanates from his forehead, a red **OM** emanates from his throat, and a blue **HUNG** emanates from his heart. These seed syllables represent his Body, Speech and Mind respectively, and are integrated with your body, speech and mind so you become as Drenpa Namkha. That is what Guru Yoga means. Through your devotion, this also establishes a connection with the teaching. It is important to do this at the beginning.

Don't read any prayers or mantras or anything when you visualize Drenpa Namkha, but between the sessions of Guru Yoga you can recite this prayer and the mantras[17] as much as you can, and that will be very beneficial. That is preparation.

After you have completed this visualization, you still see everything as you did before. This is how your own consciousness is working. Everything is like this – good things, bad things, everything is created in this way, through thinking. For now we are talking about Guru Yoga and Guru Yoga is also created by you, by your imagination – if you open your eyes you can't see anything

---

their Relation to the Teachings of a Central Asian Buddha, (Kathmandu: Vajra Publications, 2008), pp. 144-148.

[16] Tib. thang ka.

[17] See p. 171.

different. Don't expect to see something or hear something special, that is not so easy. The main thing is devotion; that is important. Your devotion must be stable, not just something you remember once or twice. Keep your devotion throughout your whole life. It is very, very important, it is a connection.

Introduction to the Natural State

Looking back towards the thought [sems' tshol]

You can do this exercise by looking back towards a thought, your devotion or even your visualization, as all these things are created by your own perception and consciousness. Just look at that thought, that perception. When you try to look at it, nothing remains. If you open your eyes, even if your visualization was very clear indeed, you will still only see the normal things of phenomenal existence, you can't see anything special. If you look back towards your thought, there is nothing to see and what remains is an unspeakable state. Don't follow what I am saying – look into that state you have heard about. Do this yourself. Don't follow your continuous thoughts or whatever you see. Just after you look back towards a thought then that thought is no longer stable, it no longer exists, and what remains is an unspeakable state. It is quite clear. It is very, very important for you to have a clear understanding and experience of this before you receive these teachings.

Look at the first thought and look back at who is looking at it. They both disappear simultaneously and nothing remains, yet you are not unconscious. The state which goes on afterwards is the Unspeakable State. That means that your presence is clear but it is impossible to explain what is clear as there is no thinking; you do not judge anything as being emptiness, clarity, this or that – nothing. It is not possible to explain this, yet your Presence is clear so that means you are alive. It seems fresh. You are not thinking. You must realize this State by yourself. Don't mix this with any mental activity. Don't think: 'This is empty;' or 'This is clear.' Look at the thought. It disappears completely. That should be clear to you. If you are not very clear about this, these teachings won't work for you at all. But if you understand that State clearly then you can correct yourself when you hear them and what I say will be suitable for you, compatible with your experience, so you will be able to understand. There are three aspects here: you receive the teaching, you have your experience, and you listen to what I am saying, and these three[18] must be in agreement. Then you are perfect, ready to begin to understand the Dzogchen View. It is not

[18] Tib. thos bsam sgom gsum.

complete yet, but this is the beginning of understanding.

Presence and Clarity

When you look towards a thought, the thought itself disappears. Who is watching disappears at the same time. After everything has disappeared, your experience[19] and presence[20] are quite clear, and this means that this state is not like unconsciousness. It says here that this clarity[21] is like a shining sun – there is no need to add anything else, it is self-clear[22] to the practitioner. What is this presence? It is an unspeakable State, so when we say it is 'clear' that doesn't refer to seeing things clearly. Neither can you compare it to the sun shining or to electric light; don't think it is clear in that sense. The presence is very clear to the practitioner who has the experience. It says here: 'Don't expect to add anything or find any other place which is clear.' For example, if you light up a lamp you don't need to add any other light to see it – the lamp itself is clear. So that means that this clarity is not comparable to any other clarity; it is self-clear, or clear to a practitioner who understands this presence. You have to understand this.

This is not like ordinary clarity as there are no judgements whatsoever because it is not influenced by perception or consciousness. It is like a crystal ball; all kinds of visions and reflections appear when you look into a crystal ball, but the ball itself doesn't change. That is similar. It is clear and shining but it cannot be explained. That is the example for how reflections come from the Nature without changing the Nature itself. This presence is called Nature, and Nature is like the crystal ball – many reflections can come from there, they appear there, yet there is no change to the Nature itself.

Meditation

After thoughts have been liberated, remain in that state, and that is meditation.[23] There is no object, no subject. In Dzogchen, meditation means not thinking. Just leave it as it is. As long as you abide in that State, that is pure meditation.

This Nature is also like a wish-fulfilling jewel. All kinds of things – good or bad – arise from there and the Nature, the Base,[24]

[19] Tib. nyams.
[20] Tib. rig pa.
[21] Tib. gsal ba.
[22] Tib. rang gsal.
[23] Tib. sgom pa.
[24] Tib. gzhi.

does not change. How does everything appear? You can see this very clearly. When you are keeping still, quietly having a rest, and not planning anything, not busy with your thinking mind, thoughts still appear spontaneously even though you are deliberately trying to remain quiet. Where do those thoughts come from? You have to think about this. They don't come from anywhere outside, nor from anywhere inside. They don't come from your body, speech or mind. You cannot recognize anything as the source, yet it is clear that a thought comes. So where is it coming from at that moment? From the Nature itself; it comes from its own Nature. If you don't follow the train of thought, if you don't try to stop it or do anything with it, but if instead you just leave it, then it will soon disappear by itself. Where does it disappear to? There is no trace at all. It comes and goes itself, like a wave rising from water into water and subsiding back to water. The wave *is* water! In the same way, all kinds of thoughts are the Nature and the Nature comes up as thought. So if you don't follow thoughts or try to stop them, but if instead you just leave them as they are, then that is the Nature. That is practising and realizing the Natural State.

Any kind of thought can arise and may be related to the past, present or future, but if you neither follow nor stop them, they come, stay a while, and disappear by themselves. If you don't follow them but just leave them to disappear, then you are always abiding clearly in the Nature itself. That is called Awareness or Rigpa.[25]

This Nature is described as Purity,[26] Clarity,[27] Unification,[28] Perfection[29] and although it encompasses all these, you don't need to recognize each aspect when you abide in the Natural State. Just remain in the Nature. Never try to integrate this State with any mental activity because if you think something like 'this is right' or 'this is wrong' or 'I have to do this,' then it looks as though you are focusing a little, and so that is not the right way. This is completely beyond thought; you must bear that in mind.

Correcting deviations in your meditation

It is easy to fall into one mistake in particular. When you abide in this state beyond thought, there is a presence, and the Unspeakable State is clear. However, if you remain in this clarity for a long time,

[25] Tib. rig pa.
[26] Tib. ka dag.
[27] Tib. gsal ba.
[28] Tib. dbyer med, gnyis med.
[29] Tib. lhun grub.

you may quite soon begin relaxing, growing calmer and calmer. It looks as though you are very relaxed, so you may think that this is good meditation because it brings bliss or some nice sensations. But at that time it is up to you as the practitioner to realize that you are in fact losing the aspect of clarity. So this is delusion. You alone can judge and recognize this. If you realize you are losing your clarity, you should stop meditating and either look back towards the thought which is waiting to liberate and then keep on again in the Natural State once it has liberated, or, if you are more familiar with this State, you don't need to look back towards a thought; you can simply remember and then you are OK, you are back in the Nature, real Nature. It is up to you, the practitioner, to make this distinction. This is an important point. You can spend a lot of time in this kind of mistaken meditation but it is completely deluded, it is integrated with dullness. It happens quite often. Many meditators make this mistake and think that this very calm state is great meditation or something.

Integrating meditation with activities

The advanced practitioner

As you become increasingly familiar with the State and more stable, walking or moving your body in any way doesn't disturb your realization of the Nature. It is the same when thoughts come. Nothing disturbs your own realization of the Nature so it doesn't matter whether you are sitting, or practising in the country, or in the town, or going some place. At this stage you need to have more time to practise so that your awareness of the Nature becomes really stable. Once you are stable enough, there is no need to search for any particular quiet, solitary place to practise. It doesn't make much difference where you are. Although everything appears as normal – colours, forms, tastes etc – and you can move your body or use any objects, your experience is completely integrated with your own Nature. The text says that no matter where an advanced practitioner like this finds himself, no matter what he does, everything is as Buddha's work because he is not influenced by thoughts at all. Anything which is integrated with thinking, with thought, consciousness or perception, is impure. That even includes the visualization of Yidams,[30] or Kyerim, Dzogrim[31] in High Tantra; from the point of view of Dzogchen, this is all impure because it is connected with consciousness.

[30] Tib. yi dam.
[31] Tib. bskyed rim, rdzogs rim.

As for a practitioner who is not so far advanced, sometimes you are concentrating in the Nature or meditating but thoughts appear spontaneously. How can you convert these thoughts and integrate them? There are three categories:

The fairly advanced practitioner

This is someone who has gone quite far along the way of becoming a good meditator, who is already very stable in Basic Nature. Thoughts still arise and he can see them come, but he never blocks them or follows them, he just leaves them. So his thoughts don't cause any damage or disturb him at all. That is the method of a practitioner who is not so far advanced but who is still a good one.

The middling practitioner

You can see that your meditation is not so stable, that thoughts come while you are keeping in the Equi-point[32] of Nature. You can see the thoughts, you realize they are arising and you know that you don't need to follow them or stop them, yet it is quite hard to come back to the Nature. At that time you have to concentrate and remember not to follow thoughts; you have to be kind of careful.[33] That is the method of the second practitioner, the method of dealing with thoughts which appear continuously.

The practitioner who is not so stable

As for the third practitioner who is less stable in the Nature, thoughts come and they can disturb you, so it looks as though you forget your own concentration with the Nature. This is especially the case for beginners. Soon after this happens, you realize that you are being disturbed by thoughts. At that time, just look at the thought itself and it again liberates back to the Nature. Initially, beginners always have to be careful not to follow or block any kind of thoughts which arise. Soon afterwards, a thought comes and it disturbs your meditation. When you realize that your meditation is disturbed by thoughts, just look back towards the thought again and it liberates by itself.

There is a parable about this here. It says that it is like a kingfisher catching fish; when a fish comes, the bird picks it up at once. Similarly, when thoughts come, remember the Nature. You

[32] Tib. mnyam bzhag.

[33] This may appear contradictory; however, the reference here is not to ordinary thinking but to Tib. dran pa, mindful awareness and Tib. shes bzhin - alert watchfulness. These two are the special aids to meditation on this level.

don't need to do anything in any special way, just look towards the thought, and it liberates spontaneously. You don't need to do anything. Just remember. You are concentrating with the Nature, thoughts come, and that disturbs your realization of the Natural State. Soon afterwards, you remember that thoughts are disturbing you, and then soon after that, the thought liberates itself back to the Nature again. Beginners have to look back very often so as not to get into the habit of following or blocking thoughts, but this process is like wrestling, you see, always challenging the thoughts. Whenever a thought comes you always try to push it away or something. But just look at it – you don't need to follow it or do anything to block it. You have to be careful about that. If you follow a thought or block it, then that is the same as the disturbance itself – the blocker is also a thought, it is the same thing.

Try to just look. Sometimes there are small things, very subtle movements or mental activity which is so slight that you don't remember when it started. If this kind of thing arises, it is better not to do anything; just keep on meditating and it can liberate spontaneously into the Nature, you see. Don't always be on guard or wary that if a thought arises, it is a disturbance; if you do, then that again causes a disturbance, you see. It is better not to care. Thoughts appear continuously and you mustn't follow them when they come, but if you are always wary or warning yourself that when a thought comes, it is a disturbance or something, then that in itself is a disturbance. So the best thing is to try to be in the Natural State for longer and if disturbances do sometimes arise, just don't care very much. Leave them. It is better. Otherwise if you are always on guard and trying to check etc., this becomes a habit, you see, and it disturbs you so you can't meditate for long which in turn means you cannot become stable.

It is very much up to the practitioners themselves to take care about all these points; there is not much to explain. Many things can be happening but the main thing is not to mistake the Natural State. Keep it as it is – that is better.

Phenomenal existence

We can say that the Nature is like the ocean or water. Many different reflections appear in water, but whatever you see – forms, colours, everything – is all just water. In a similar way, all kinds of objects – our phenomenal existence, everything – appear spontaneously from the individual person's Nature. Actually, there is no general, common reality; everything appears from your own Nature. It may seem common to ourselves and others because there are many similarities between what we see and what others see, but in fact appearances don't arise from the same source or condition at all as everyone's Nature is individual. But what you have to understand here is that all objects and phenomenal existence are like a picture, a cinema picture, you see. You can see the people in a film, they are moving and it looks as though they are speaking, but if you actually look at the object, there is only the screen, nothing else. If you check carefully, all phenomena of existence are very much like a picture, you see. There is no background. You can see this from your own body or speech or mind; everything is only temporary, everything is always changing. We don't recognize this even though many things show it very clearly. We can see that time and conditions are not always stable – one day a person can be in perfect health but the next they can be very seriously ill, you see. Or one day they are rich, the next day something happens and they are very poor. That can happen. Things change easily. This shows that everything is similar to a movie, and that means that nothing can be relied upon at all. But we don't trust the real condition, we are still following the picture.

All phenomena of existence are like your very dear, close friend. One day something happens, some little thing, and your friend falls away completely and leaves you. That is very similar. None of the phenomena of existence are permanent or stable, everything is temporary. So don't have too much desire or attachment for any kind of object whatsoever. That is the example: think that all phenomena are like your very dear, very close friend, but it is not permanent. After some time your friendship is broken, something happens and you become completely estranged. That is the example, and it holds true for all phenomena of existence. You don't need to have too much desire for any kind of object.

Empty Form

Visions and all phenomena which appear are completely integrated with Empty Nature. The text gives the example of a mustard seed which always contains oil. In a similar way, all phenomena are as Empty Form[34] and never lose their Empty Nature. The Nature and the visions – whatever appears – are completely integrated with one another. Therefore it is said that all phenomena are as Empty Form. So how can they appear? It is like looking into a mirror. If you look into a mirror, it doesn't change at all even though various visions can appear there. The mirror doesn't disturb anything, the reflections don't disturb the mirror, yet whatever you see – forms,

[34] Tib. stong gzugs.

colours, everything – cannot be separated from the mirror. In a similar way, the whole of phenomenal existence is as Empty Form, Empty Forms of the Nature. Everything comes from this Nature. Nature is like the mirror and the whole of phenomenal existence is like the reflections. These two are completely inseparable and will never lose each other – visions don't lose Empty Nature nor does Empty Nature depart from visions or phenomenal existence. Therefore they are called 'illusion,' Empty Form.

Dzogchen, Refuge and Bodhichitta

While you are abiding in the Natural State, you are like a turtle kept in a plate; the turtle doesn't move at all. That is the illustration for what it is like when you are trying to remain in the Nature. Even though you are not moving from the Natural State, thoughts appear spontaneously. If you are stable in the Nature and they don't disturb your meditation, then just let them come, don't stop them or do anything. You can see thoughts arising, but leave them, and they will soon disappear by themselves. They are like birds flying in space – they don't leave any traces behind. It doesn't matter which thoughts come, if you are quite stable in the Nature, just let them come because no matter how many thoughts arise, they don't damage anything as they don't leave any trace. If they don't leave any traces then that means they don't produce any karmic causes. The trace is like a karmic cause. If you haven't realized Basic Nature then any thought which comes will leave a trace, a karmic cause, whether you are following and acting upon it or not.

Usually we talk about Bodhichitta[35] and Refuge[36] and say that they are the best practices, but here it says that anything we practise or develop using thoughts – such as creating the visualization of Yidams, reciting mantras and so on – cannot be better than simply remaining in the Natural State. Many people who have been listening and following the teachings for a while and have always heard about Refuge and Bodhichitta may have doubts about this, you see, because here it suddenly says that this Natural State is beyond everything. That can cause some sort of mess or confusion, you see, as it is different and seems contradictory. So it is important to explain this a little bit.

You should not think that this text or the Dzogchen View is only talking about emptiness or nihilism. Dzogchen never thinks anything, neither good nor bad, nothing. This Dzogchen View is not comparable to any other view because it has the aspect of

[35] Tib. byang chub sems.
[36] Tib. skyabs 'gro.

Perfection, which we call Lhundrub.[37] It is very important to know this. How is it perfected or Lhundrub? What does it mean? If you look at milk, for instance, you know that it contains butter but you can't see it; you can't recognize anything in the milk or fully comprehend how the butter can be there. But if you churn the milk, the butter appears. That is the parable for the Natural State. 'Perfection' means that whatever is needed can manifest.

For example, if a Dzogchen practitioner has advanced very deeply or highly in the Natural State and some kind of help or act of compassion is called for, the practitioner will act spontaneously, you see, if it is possible. Nothing is blocked or negated. It is the same for Refuge, Bodhichitta and so on – everything is perfected within the Natural State. The Ten Paramitas – generosity and so on[38] – are all there, nothing is rejected. If someone practises the Natural State and is advanced, he doesn't need to take some special vow not to kill or tell lies and so on, but even so he will never cause harm. He won't kill or steal because he is not influenced by any wishes or intentions, nothing like that. So, from the point of view of Dzogchen, there is no rejection of or contradiction with other views – that is called 'Perfection.' It is rather difficult to trust, you see. Perfection. Dzogchen. It looks as though everything is nihilism, but in fact the Dzogchen View has nothing to accept, nothing to reject. It is not against anything. Whatever is needed can appear spontaneously as reflections appear in a mirror.

[37] Tib. lhun gdrub.

[38] Tib. phar phyin bcu: sbyin pa - generosity; tshul khrims - moral discipline; bzod pa - patience; brtson 'grus - determination; bsam gtan - contemplation; stobs - power or perseverance; snying rje - compassion; smon lam - prayer of aspiration; thabs - method or dedication (bsngo ba); shes rab - wisdom.

Thirty Signs and Meanings of Mogyud, the Female Lineage [Mo brgyud brda don sum bcu pa]

So far I have been explaining about Dzogchen because here, in this teaching, the foundation is to realize what the Natural State is and what its qualities are. If you just keep quiet without knowing these kinds of things, you might think you are meditating, but your meditation is not so useful and is just passing time. You yourself must make sure that you have understood the Natural State properly. The teachings which follow are all about what the Nature is and how to practise it, so the next steps are not of much use for you if you don't have a clear understanding of the base.

This Dzogchen View was practised by male and female practitioners alike, and this is the foundation. All the Dakinis[39] in this lineage are Dzogchen practitioners and one after the other, they transmitted the teachings, handing them down from one woman to the next. They received the teachings, practised them and finally, all the women in this lineage achieved Rainbow Body.[40]

[39] Zzng. dha ki ni. Tib. mkha' 'gro - literally 'sky-goer'.

[40] Tib. 'ja' lus. There are three main types of Rainbow Body. The highest level is called Tib. 'ja' lus 'pho ba chen po - the Rainbow Body of the Great Transfer. At this level a practitioner becomes a complete Buddha in his or her very body. Unnoticed by others, the physical body of such a practitioner is transformed into the essence of the five elements, the five pure lights (Tib. 'od lnga); such a person does not manifest any signs of death. This kind of being can disappear and reappear on this mundane plane at any point in time or space in response to the needs of those seeking the path of realization. The early Masters of the *Zhang Zhung Nyengyud* (Tib. Zhang zhung snyan rgyud), as well as yogis from other lineages of Bönpo Dzogchen, such as Tsewang Rigdzin (Tib. Tshe dbang Rig 'dzin), all achieved this level of realization. Guru Padmasambhava and Vimalamitra of the Buddhist Dzogchen tradition are also said to have achieved this level of realization. The second type of Rainbow Body is when the practitioner's body dissolves into the rainbow light of the essence of the five elements at the time of death without leaving any physical remains behind. This level of realization is sometimes called the Light Body or Luminous Body (Tib. 'od sku, 'od lus). The third level is when the practitioner's body shrinks at the time of death until ultimately only hair and nails are left; these are considered to be external to the body as pain is not felt when they are cut. Sometimes practitioners do not attain full dissolution into the essence of the elements and their body shrinks to a greater or lesser extent. In such cases, although the practitioner has a high level of realization, he or she has not quite completed Thögal (Tib. thod rgal) practice during their lifetime. After Namdak, Yongdzin Lopön

Why are we talking about these Dakinis? The Dzogchen *Yetri Thasel* was transmitted from Dharmakaya, Sambhogakaya and Nirmanakaya[41] to many different types of sentient beings and although sentient beings generally fall into two categories, male and female, the real Nature is the same in all of them. Sometimes we read explanations of male and female Dharmakaya, and even though there is no separation on the Nature's side, we quite often explain two aspects of this Nature: the clarity aspect and the emptiness aspect. These are two facets of the same Nature. The empty aspect is sometimes called 'female Dharmakaya,'[42] or in our words, Satrig Ersang.[43] That means Loving Wisdom Goddess. She is the source, she introduced the Natural State to sentient beings.

As there are two types of practitioner, male and female, there are two lineages, male and female. There always were and there always will be many female practitioners and many female lineages, but they are not usually listed in the texts. I don't know what the reason for that is. This time I am teaching from the female lineage.

How did this lineage start? The text first explains how the highest Dakini was emanated: Dharmakaya Satrig Ersang, the Loving Goddess of Wisdom, emanated a Dakini called Beautiful Goddess or Khandro Dzema Yiwongma, a Sambhogakaya form. As Satrig Ersang is a Buddha – Dharmakaya – ordinary beings cannot see her; only Buddhas themselves can see each other. So Satrig Ersang emanated this Beautiful Dakini Dzema Yiwongma, who is a Sambhogakaya form, in order to control all wrathful and peaceful Khandro.[44] As Sambhogakaya forms can only be seen by high practitioners, only such beings could listen and receive teachings from Dzema Yiwongma, so she emanated a Nirmanakaya in India – Gyagargyi Khandro Ulishak – and transmitted this teaching to her. That is the third Dakini. So Ulishak, the Nirmanakaya form, received this teaching from Dzema Yiwongma, the Sambhogakaya form. She gave Ulishak a Dzogchen text which was written in blue ink on a copper plate which she took miraculously from space. Ulishak's language was Sanskrit, so when she received this text from Dzema Yiwongma she could read and translate it into Sanskrit.

Tenzin, transc. & ed. Ermakova, C. & Ermakov, D. *Masters of the Zhang Zhung Nyengyud*, pp. 19-20, Footnote 27.

[41] Tib. bon sku, sprul sku, rdzogs sku.

[42] Tib. Kun tu bZang mo.

[43] For Tibetan, Wylie transliteration and translation of the names see *The Khandro Cycle of Mogyud* p. 19.

[44] Tib. mkha' 'gro.

It was originally written in some other language, but this text doesn't specify which one.

There are two components to this text: direct teaching with a sign; and a kind of commentary on the meaning of the sign or symbol. First of all the sign was shown and then afterwards the Dakini explained what it meant, and gave an interpretation of the sign. That is how it was transmitted

Khandro Yoga [mkha' 'gro rnal 'byor]

Before we read the teaching of each Dakini, it is very important to practise Guru Yoga. Visualize the Dakini and meditate with the Natural State according to her teachings.

Body posture

You should sit in the five-pointed body posture as usual, with your legs crossed, spine straight, your two hands in the *mudra* of equipoise,[45] your neck a little bent, and your eyes gazing straight ahead on a level with your nose. Don't close your mouth, just let the breath come and go in the normal way. That is the body posture.

Visualization

Try to visualize the Dakini as clearly as you can. Whether she is bigger or smaller depends on whatever is convenient for you. First of all look at the picture, it gives you a brief idea of her features. But don't think that the Dakini you visualize is like this; she is not merely a painting, not always hanging out on the *thangka*. She is completely luminous light, pure, and full of knowledge. She is not only a statue without feeling or movement, you see. She is alive, completely alive, and full of knowledge.

When you have completed the visualization of her whole body, focus there as long as you can.Then receive the three elements from her in the same way as usual. Wisdom fire emanates from her heart level and, entering the crown of your head, it burns away all your defilements. Then wisdom water flows from the Dakini's heart and washes away any defilements which are left. Finally, visualize that wisdom wind comes to you from the Dakini's heart and blows away any remaining impurities. So you are completely purified, ready to receive the blessings of the Dakinis.

Then after this, you receive the three seed syllables which represent the Dakini's body, speech and mind. These come to you as a white **A**, red **OM** and blue **HUNG** which emanate from the Dakini's forehead, neck and chest respectively and are integrated

[45] Tib. mnyam bzhag gi phyag rgya.

with you, so you become full of blessings and *siddhi*.[46]

That is real, practical initiation or empowerment. 'Empowerment' means that the Dakini's knowledge is transferred from her to you, and you receive it through your devotion. That is what taking empowerment really means.

After this, as I read the teaching, keep in the Natural State, and meditate for at least ten minutes on what the Dakini taught here. Don't just follow words when you meditate; if you do, your meditation will be disturbed.

Satrig Ersang

[46] Tib. grub.

1. Dzema Yiwongma
First of all, Dzema Yiwongma showed Ulishak the sign, the rope of light from space.

Then she explained the meaning:

The Natural State is called the Nature of Bodhichitta. It is also called Dharmakaya, Nature Dharmakaya. Nature is Dharmakaya which is not formed as the five aggregates,[47] nor is there any increase or decrease. This Nature is not newly born, it knows neither death nor birth. There is no sickness, it cannot be killed or made alive; there is nothing special which can be explained. This Nature cannot be separated into Clarity and Emptiness; there is no distinction. In particular there is neither object nor subject. All phenomena of existence are integrated with this Nature. This Nature is the Unspeakable State. It is the base, everything comes from it and abides in it. That is called Basic Dharmakaya.

That is the meaning of this sign.

2. Gyagar Khandro Ulishak
After Ulishak[48] received the teachings, she showed the sign or symbol to Walmoza Namkha Wökyi Gyalmo, the Queen of Light.

Then she explained the meaning:

The Nature of Bodhichitta is indestructible. This is the final goal of Dharmakaya which neither increases nor decreases. It is unchangeable throughout the three times of past, present and future. It is called 'stable as the swastika.' This is the Base of all Nirvana and Samsara which never deviates; therefore it is called 'the unchangeable, indestructible banner.'

That is the meaning. To clarify this: it is not possible to destroy or disturb the Natural State at all.

---

[47] Tib. phung po lnga.
[48] Yongdzin Rinpoche explained that since Ulishak is the Nirmanakaya aspect of Dzema Yiwongma, they are represented by one image on the *thankga*.

Dzema Yiwongma
Gyagar Khandro Ulishak

3. Walmoza Namkha Wökyi Gyalmo

This time it is Razhagza Salwai Yingchyugma who received the teaching. First of all her teacher, Walmoza Namkha Wökyi Gyalmo, showed the sign. It was just to stand up in a simple way for a little while.

The meaning is that the Natural State does not rely on any cause or any kind of support; there is nothing like that. It is completely pure Nature. That is what this sign shows.

As for the teaching itself:

The Natural State itself is naturally called Buddha Nature or Ye Sanggyepa[49] which means the 'Purified Nature of Buddha.' In general, there are three kinds of Buddha – Dharmakaya, Sambhogakaya and Nirmanakaya, the Three Kayas. Within these there are Basic Dharmakaya, Path Dharmakaya and Result Dharmakaya. The name is the same but the quality and the circumstances are completely different.

Nature itself is completely pure, so that is called Nature-Buddha. This Nature does not rely on any cause or support. It is beyond thought. It is Unchangeable Swastika Bodhichitta. But this Natural State is not independent; it is connected with beings.

A being has body, speech and mind, and nothing is created; just integrate with Empty Nature. You have to understand that, for that is Nature. We don't need to visualize anything, change anything or do anything. We just have to realize what it is.

Nature encompasses both visions and emptiness. It is beyond nihilism and eternalism. Although many terms are used, these are all created by the individual or impure thinking.

This Nature is Clarity, Emptiness and Unification. That is called Self-Originated Kaya or Ku, Rangjyung Ku,[50] Self-Originated Body.

---

[49] Tib. ye sangs rgyas pa.

[50] Tib. rang 'byung sku.

Walmoza Namkha Wökyi Gyalmo

4. Razhagza Salwa Yingchyugma
Salwai Yingchyugma showed the symbol and transmitted the teachings to Zhangzhungza Wökyi Lama.

Nature is not covered by any obscurations at all. This Empty Nature is the Nature of Mind which is clear and empty. If you look there, there is nothing material, nothing to be seen. There is nothing in this State which can be explained, it looks as though everything is exhausted into its own Nature. There is no object whatsoever, no subject whatsoever. This Nature is beyond all extremes such as nihilism, eternalism or anything else, as these are all created by thoughts and this goes beyond all mental concepts. What you should do is abide in the Nature as long as you can and then all phenomena of existence – including your own body, speech and mind – are liberated to Nature; all of them. So there is no particular object of meditation, nothing. Simply remain in this Presence.

Razhagza Salwa Yingchyugma

5. Zhangzhungza Wökyi Lama

Zhangzhungza Wökyi Lama taught Dongcham Kharmokyong. This lady comes from Dong which may be in the southern part of Tibet.

She showed the symbol or sign:

The symbol means that thoughts are all liberated back to the Nature. That means that all phenomena are as empty form. The sign is not merely something special which the Dakini demonstrates; it symbolizes that everything is just self-liberated back to Empty Nature.

The concluding teachings which Zhangzhungza Wökyi Lama taught Dongcham Kharmokyong are as follows:

The Nature is like space. Space is only an example. But real Nature is the Pure Nature-Buddha which is clear, empty and beyond material things. This is called awareness. Awareness has neither centre nor edge, it cannot be measured, there are no forms, nothing. This Nature is beyond all objects. It is called Empty Dharmakaya. It is beyond all phenomena of existence. All visions which come to you are integrated with emptiness. You have to try to remain in the Nature itself; the whole of phenomenal existence is integrated with this Nature.

That is the final teaching.

Zhangzhungza Wökyi Lama

6. Dongcham Kharmokyong
Dongcham Kharmokyong taught Tagzigza – that means that this Dakini comes from Tagzig. Her name is Manggye Salgyema.
The symbol or sign shows light in the space.

The concluding teachings Dongcham Kharmokyong gave to the Tagzig Dakini Manggye Salgyema are as follows:

It is difficult to check the Natural State because everything is pure. It is beyond being spoken of or thought of. Phenomenal existence arises as a vision which is already Empty Form. Whatever appears is primordially integrated with Empty Nature. Everything is Dharmakaya, Nature-Dharmakaya, but it is difficult to know and show this. All phenomena of existence are naturally liberated to the Nature and nothing needs to be removed or avoided; nothing. Everything is naturally pure Buddha. All kinds of visions are miraculous manifestations. They are called the energy or Tsal of awareness.[51]

Those are the concluding teachings which Manggye Salgyema was given after she had received all Dzogchen teachings.

[51] Tib. rig pa'i rtsal.

Dongcham Kharmokyong

7. Tagzigza Manggye Salgyema
Tagzigza Manggye Salgyema taught Urgyenza Rigngen Düdtsikyong, a Dakini from Urgyen.
First of all the sign is like this, with both hands holding each other under the left leg, under the knee.

The concluding teachings are:

From the limitless beginning up until now, the Natural State is and was like the vast expanse of space. Visions such as mandalas, divinities, colours, or forms arise non-stop. Many things can appear, but nothing is far from the Nature itself. No matter what visions arise, they never disturb this Nature; it will always be stable and clear, and that is unchangeable. It is as though sealed. There is no change, no movement, nothing special, yet it is always that State.

Tagzigza Manggye Salgyema

8. Urgyenza Rigngen Düdtsikyong

Urgyenza Rigngen Düdtsikyong showed the sign to Gyagar Phamthingza Thuchenma. You lie down like this in the lion posture, stretch both legs and your left hand is placed on your thigh.

Then she commented and gave the final concluding teachings:

It is impossible for Semnyi,[52] the Natural State, to focus on any kind of objects, nor is there any subject. This is the Nature of Dharmakaya which is beyond any activities. It has no cause, no support, nothing. It is beyond anything else. This Nature has no colour, no form, and no size. It has no object whatsoever. We cannot speak of it as appearing, disappearing, being destroyed, or dying. This Nature has no antidotes at all. It has no support, no cause. There is nothing to focus on. This Nature is vast. It is emptiness, clarity and unification. This is the Nature of Mind; it is as space.

That is all.

[52] Tib. sems nyid – 'nature of mind.'

Urgyenza Rigngen Düdtsikyong

9. Gyagar Phamthingza Thuchenma

Phamthingza transmitted the teachings to Gyaza Salwa Wödron. Gyaza means Chinese.

First of all, she showed the sign of Phowa,[53] transference to the wrathful Yidam. There is no special posture or sign to show here as it is a kind of Phowa, the transference of a practitioner's consciousness which becomes integrated with a wrathful Yidam. Don't think that there is some Yidam which exists independently out there. When you do Phowa, you visualize a Yidam, divinity or Dakini as independently present in front of you, then your consciousness is transferred into the divinity and integrated with it. So it looks as though one person's mind were transferring to another person or being, but that is not possible. You can't transfer consciousness and integrate two people's minds, joining them together as one thing, although it may seem like this when it is described very briefly. When we explain these teachings it seems as though we transfer our consciousness to somebody else, but that is not right. What it means is that we have to realize the Nature of Mind and that is your Nature, not anyone else's. Your Nature will never break away or go away from you, but very often you don't recognize it. There are many methods to help you recognize your Nature, but in our tradition, there are four categories, especially when you take a tantric initiation: external, internal, secret and esoteric. The latter means complete realization of the Natural State. At the time of the first initiation you are trying to realize the Natural State. The second initiation is a kind of blessing. The third is more to do with an individual practitioner having special experiences, and the fourth is the introduction to the Natural State itself. When you receive this final initiation, you will realize that the Natural State is complete and perfect. 'Perfect' means that you have to know this clearly, not merely thinking 'it is supposed to be like this.' First of all, you have to experience the Natural State yourself. Then secondly, your experience and the text have to agree. Thirdly, a qualified, experienced Master introduces and explains the Natural State to you. If your experience, the text and the Master's explanation all completely agree and you fully understand, then that is called 'introduction.' Whoever has this trust and knowledge has received the initiation. That is generally what Phowa means, but in this case Phowa is only used as a symbol.

The Chinese Dakini Salwa Wödron received these concluding teachings from Phamthingza:

---

[53] Tib. 'pho ba.

All phenomena of existence appear from Awareness into Awareness and are themselves Awareness. They appear clearly. This Clarity is much brighter and clearer than the light of a thousand suns and moons. This great light is integrated with every consciousness and perception, and purifies the darkness of ignorance. No matter how deep ignorance may be, it can be purified instantly. Once the darkness of obscurations and defilements has all been purified, that is called the Nature Buddha. This Nature Buddha has purified the root of Samsara.[54] It doesn't matter whether it is an early Buddha or a new Buddha; anyone who achieves Buddhahood has equally purified the root and is equally in the Natural State. That is called "the Three Times come into one."

Gyagar Phamthingza Thuchenma

[54] Here Rinpoche refers to Tib. ye sangs rgyas pa - 'the primordial Buddha' synonymous with Tib. gnas lugs - the Natural State, which is the Nature of Mind - Tib. sems nyid - and is primordially pure and unsullied.

10. Gyaza Salwa Wödron

Gyaza Salwa Wödron transmitted the teaching to Yorpoza Drime Dangdenma. Yorpo is a village in the southern part of central Tibet, near Lhasa. The Dakini's personal name is Drime Dangdenma. She again showed a sign, the Phowa of Natural Clear Light. That is similar to what we explained about Phowa above but there is no visible symbol to show.

The teachings she received are:

The Natural State is like great nectar or medicine. External phenomenal existence as well as internal sentient beings – whoever, wherever they may be – are connected with this. Whatever appears is a kind of nectar and medicine. Whatever appears, whether good or bad, is sealed by the Natural State. Nothing exists beyond the Natural State, and the Natural State is great nectar. How can we abide in this, practise and know this? It is impossible to know it by means of consciousness or perception; simply leave it as it is, vast and empty, open and free. Leave it. Don't try to grasp or perceive anything – that is nectar. If you do this, you have received the great nectar-medicine of Dharmakaya which can purify and clean everything. Obscurations, defilements, miseries, sufferings – these are all purified. Therefore it is called nectar, amrita.

That is the teaching.

Gyaza Salwa Wödron

11. Yorpoza Drime Dangdenma

Yorpoza transmitted the teachings to Chöza Wökyi Dzutrultön. This surname, Chöza, is similar to a Chöza who will come later on but it is a different person. The text doesn't mention where this Chöza comes from but she is supposed to be a southern Tibetan. Her personal name is Wökyi Dzutrultön. Yorpoza showed the symbol of touching her left thigh with her right hand and twisting her body.

The meaning of this is the concluding teaching:

The meaning is the Empty Nature, the example, or Pe,[55] is space, and the sign is the Natural State. So that is the example, the meaning and the sign. The personal Natural State is the sign. These three categories together show that the Natural State has no beginning. It is an unspeakable State which cannot be defined, so it is called Dagmepa[56] – self-less. It encompasses all phenomenal existence, both internal and external.

This Natural State or Empty Nature can be likened to a lotus which is born and grows from dirty, muddy water yet it is utterly pure, clear and clean when it blossoms. In a similar way, it doesn't matter whether the Natural State is integrated with emotions, anger or desire or anything else, it will always be clear and pure, the unification of Clarity and Emptiness. The Natural State is perfected with this. All external and internal faults are purified naturally within the Nature itself. It doesn't make much difference for the Natural State itself whether you realize this or not. The Natural State is always pure and equally encompasses any kind of consciousness or phenomenon.

The Natural State is like a wish-fulfilling jewel because any phenomenon or vision can arise from it. There is no choice between good or bad, right or wrong; anything can come from this Nature. This is called Awareness. The Natural State is Awareness and Nature, and it is like a wish-fulfilling jewel.

This Nature is also like a rainbow; you can see all kinds of visions but you cannot use them. This applies to the whole of phenomenal existence, both internal and external: you can see or hear everything but the background is empty. There is nothing which exists concretely at all, nothing whatsoever. Maybe we think that our property and everything is real. It looks real but it is

[55] Tib. dpe.
[56] Tib. bdag med pa - i.e. absence of self.

only temporary, only something we have created as real;[57] it is not naturally real at all. There is always evidence of this. For example, I quite often say how much everything changes from morning until noon. Everything changes, not just your own conditions, but externally, too. That shows there is nothing whatsoever which exists permanently. Everything is changing, moving, going, passing. Yet still we don't trust what that means. This impermanence shows that everything is Empty Form, that nothing exists inherently, that nothing is trustable. All phenomena are visions, and they are completely integrated with Empty Nature. So that is called Dharmakaya, Nature-Dharmakaya.

But we don't know this unless we follow and listen to the teachings seriously.

Yorpoza Drime Dangdenma

[57] I.e. the 'reality,' concreteness of things is only created by our mind.

12. Chöza Wökyi Dzutrultön

Chöza Wökyi Dzutrultön transmitted the teachings to Dzutrul Natsogtön from Drusha.

The sign or symbol shows the six chakras: the crown, neck, heart, navel, secret and feet chakras.

The meaning of the teachings is:

The Nature of the Natural State is Emptiness. There is nothing which can be seen materially, no substance, no characteristics, nothing at all. Moreover, it is beyond the extremes of nihilism or any kind of philosophical views such as eternalism, existence, non-existence. This Nature cannot be explained as being this or that. Nor can it be explained temporarily as Clarity, Emptiness or anything else. It is impossible to explain it, yet you can say whatever you wish to about it. Nevertheless, it cannot be comprehended by thinking. That means it is beyond all philosophical schools, beyond thinking, beyond existence. This Nature does not apprehend any of the six objects through perception, not at all, neither does it grasp at 'self.'[58] Moreover, this Nature has no sides such as East, North and so on, neither has it colours or forms; there is nothing which perception is able to recognize. It is just itself, beyond all perceptions and consciousness. That is the Nature.

That is the concluding teaching.

[58] Tib. bdag 'dzin.

Chöza Wökyi Dzutrultön

13. Drushaza Dzutrul Natsogtön

Drushaza transmitted the teachings to Lunggyenza Nangwa Datönma. The sign is connected with Luminous Light Wisdom, so there is nothing special to show.

The concluding teaching Drushaza taught Lunggyenza Nangwa Datönma is:

This Nature neither increases nor decreases. It is not possible to liberate or delude it; nothing can damage it. The Nature itself is always Great Perfection. It cannot be explained using examples taken from phenomenal existence nor can we say it is nihilism or eternalism. There is nothing which can be explained. It is beyond all these extremes or views. It is itself the perfected one. It can be the base of all things, and everything appears as a vision.[59] This Perfection has several qualities. Even though both pure and impure things can appear, the latter are only temporarily connected with Nature; Nature itself is not influenced by impure visions. Here, 'impure' means anything connected with thought and perception. As you deepen your practice of Trekchö[60] and combine this with the methods of Thögal,[61] visions will arise, and these are all pure because they are not integrated with any kind of thought. It doesn't matter what arises – emotions, Bodhichitta, Refuge, good thoughts, bad thoughts – anything integrated with any appearance is something impure – that seems contradictory! The whole of phenomenal existence – internal, external, everything – is inextricably integrated with the great Natural State. All kinds of visions come from Rigpa Yeshe,[62] everything appears from Wisdom Awareness. No matter what comes from Wisdom Awareness, nothing whatsoever can exist inherently. We all think that everything is concrete, reality, but we have merely created that by ourselves. So the creator is called ignorance.

These are the concluding teachings.

[59] Tib. snang ba.
[60] Tib. khregs mchod.
[61] Tib. thod rgal.
[62] Tib. rig pa ye shes.

Drushaza Dzutrul Natsogtön

14. Lunggyenza Nangwa Datönma

Lunggyenza transmitted the teachings to Menyagza Thogbebma. First of all she showed the symbol, the Rishi posture.[63] The gaze is directed towards space.

Her concluding teachings are as follows:

All kinds of visions, whatever they may be, come from Awareness. Awareness is never far from the visions, so they are inseparable from the Nature, Wisdom Awareness. This Nature and Awareness are beyond thought and conceptual grasping. As the Nature itself is Wisdom Awareness, all visions – pure or impure – are equally integrated with Wisdom Awareness. When you realize that all phenomena of existence, internal or external, are as Empty Form, and provided you have fully understood what Empty Form means, you will see that there is nothing which exists inherently, nothing is real. Even thoughts, including validated knowledge,[64] are all as Empty Form and are not to be trusted. This Nature or Awareness is said to be the place of liberation.[65] How are all phenomena of existence liberated? They are all encompassed within Wisdom Awareness so they liberate like waves which come from water and go back into water. It doesn't matter whether the waves are higher or lower, they are always water. So in the same way, all kinds of visions can arise – our life is also part of these visions – and they are all called Empty Form. That is not created by anything. How do you practise? You yourself simply abide in this liberation, and all kinds of thoughts are naturally liberated. 'Liberated' means that when something appears spontaneously, you leave it without following it, without stopping it and without adding anything. Don't do anything. Just leave it. It will soon liberate by itself. After this liberation there is the Unspeakable State. That shows the result of Liberation or the Natural State.

That is the teaching.

---

[63] One of the main Thögal positions.

[64] Tib. tshad ma - valid cognition.

[65] Tib. thar pa.

Lunggyenza Nangwa Datönma

15. Menyagza Thogbebma

This Dakini is from Menyag. Menyag is another name for Tanguut, an ancient country to the east of Tibet which has now disappeared as it was conquered in the days of Chingis Khaan.[66] Menyagza Thogbebma transmitted the teachings to Urgyenza Namkhacham.[67] The symbol is the light of awareness coming from space, from the Natural State. These lights are not ordinary lights; it means that any kind of visions or lights come from Empty Nature, from space. That is the sign.

As for the teaching itself:

The Natural State is beyond any kind of substance or material thing. Everything is permeated by the Natural State and is seen by the Nature itself, nothing exists inherently. The whole of phenomenal existence – external, internal, everywhere – is equally encompassed by this Nature, by Emptiness, Clarity and Unification.

This Nature is beyond words or mental concepts; it cannot be explained directly. We have so many books and teachings but these merely use symbols. For example, if you want to show a child the moon you point your finger towards it. If the child looks along the finger they will see the moon. The moon doesn't come down to the finger, the finger doesn't reach the moon, but through the sign or symbol you can show the child the moon. In a similar way, this Nature cannot be directly explained as this or that. You can think something about what it might be, but that is only your idea and you can't see Nature at all through thinking. The only thing to do is not to think anything at all but just to carry on, to leave that Presence, whatever comes – that is the Nature. Everything comes from there, not from the brain, or the heart or your external body, nor from anywhere internally; there is no source. So if you leave everything, then that is the Base[68] or foundation. As I have already said, it is not possible to show this using any explanation, words or thoughts. Nature itself cannot be newly born, nor can it be destroyed. Therefore it is said to be like a diamond or swastika which is indestructible. That is the Nature.

---

[66] The Tanguut Hsi-hsia (Xi-xia) kingdom was destroyed by Chingis Khaan in 1225 AD. Many Tanguuts were killed but some relocated to Mongolia and Siberia where certain clans still survive to this day. See D. Ermakov, *Bø and Bön*, pp. 102-104.

[67] Rinpoche used another variation of this Khandro's name when teaching: Urgyenza Namchag Wötroma (Tib. U rgyan za gNam lcags 'Od 'phro ma). Here we use the name as it appears in the root text. See p. 115.

[68] Tib. gzhi.

Menyagza Thogbebma

16. Urgyenza Namkhacham

Urgyenza taught Shiwerza Wöthangma. I am not sure where Shiwer[69] is. First of all she showed her the sign which is the group of Thigles[70] in space. These Thigles are not visible, although maybe somebody can see them. They are not made with a camera or computer or anything like that, they are just luminous Thigles. The symbol is just looking into space, but it doesn't mean you look with your eyes – your eyes can't see this. So that is the sign.

As for the teaching:

The Natural State cannot be shown to consciousness or perception, nor can it be shown through speaking or words. This immutable Nature of Mind of the Swastika cannot be measured, nor can it be shown through examples. This Nature is itself aware of itself. It has no beginning – it is the Nature. Clarity and Emptiness can never be separated. The whole of phenomenal existence is integrated with this unity of Clarity and Emptiness. Everything which exists liberates by itself. The Nature of Mind is very special and we respect it with devotion.

That is the teaching.

[69] Tib. shi ber/shel wer.
[70] Thib thig le.

Urgyenza Namkhacham

17. Shiwerza Wöthangma

Wöthangma transmitted the teachings to Khacheza Gyändenma. This Dakini comes from Kache,[71] that means Kashmir. Urgyen and Gilgit were separate countries in the past but today they are part of Pakistan, in the Hunza where we find Taliban settlements nowadays. In early times they were Dakini places but now no more Dakinis come from there.

First of all, the symbol is that she simply sits and shows all parts of her body. Ten parts of the body are numbered. That is the sign.

The meaning or teaching is:

The Indestructible Swastika Nature has no edge, no centre; it encompasses the whole of existence as space does. This means that the Nature of Mind is unchangeable. It always remains.

It looks as though you could say it were eternal, but we cannot think of it as being eternal in the normal sense. 'Eternal' means something unchangeable which exists inherently, but this Nature cannot be comprehended by thought; you cannot think of it as eternal or as non-existent. If you could say something definite about this Nature, then that means you would be able to comprehend it using consciousness, but that would be a contradiction as it is beyond thought and perception. We are always saying it is empty, and we have to say something otherwise students wouldn't understand at all, but it is not really empty; you cannot follow the words. We say it is empty but that is just a kind of symbol; don't think it is empty. If you think it is empty then you have perceived some aspect of it; Nature cannot be apprehended by consciousness as an object, not at all. It is better not to form concepts about it. Just leave it as it is – that is the Nature.

So here it says:

It is vast like space – unchangeable, indestructible, great space. It doesn't reject anything, nor does it accept anything. It changes nothing, it does nothing. You cannot even think: 'it is like great space.' Whenever you abide in this Nature, visions continuously arise from it, so it is like a wish-fulfilling jewel. Pure or impure things can appear from the Nature, but since they are none other than pure Nature, they are in fact all pure.

---

[71] Tib. Kha che.

However, anything which becomes the subject and object of consciousness and perception is impure, as I have already said. In fact, everything comes from the Nature and is integrated with it, therefore everything is Empty Form. You don't need to visualize things as empty or something – it is better not to do anything. Just leave the Nature as it is. That is better.

Shiwerza Wöthangma

18. Khacheza Gyendenma

Khacheza Gyendenma transmitted the teachings to Gyerza, which means 'the Lady of Bön,' and her personal name is Dragchentsal. Khacheza showed the symbol of keeping her hands in equipoise.

The teaching is as follows:

The Natural State is Emptiness which has no limits. Like space, it encompasses everything. There is nothing beyond this; everything is connected with the Nature, there is nothing which exists beyond it. All kinds of emotions and the Five Poisonous Consciousnesses are like clouds, fog or mist which appear temporarily. Whatever emotions or obscurations arise are merely temporary, and the Nature will never change at all. No matter what visions appear, the Self-Awareness Wisdom remains unchanged. Anything can appear as a vision – pure or impure – but nothing is beyond this space of Empty Nature. All phenomena of existence are encompassed within this Nature and are integrated with it. They appear from the Nature into the Nature and are liberated back into the Nature. It doesn't matter whether they are pure or impure visions, good or bad thoughts – nothing makes any difference to Self-Awareness. Everything is equally integrated. The Nature never becomes clearer, it never dims; there is no change at all. Day or night, at any time, the Nature will always be the same.

That is the teaching.

Khacheza Gyendenma

19. Gyerza Dragchentsal

Gyerza Dragchentsal transmitted the teachings to Namkha Nyima Wödenma.

First of all she showed the symbol of pushing her two hands on her thigh.

As for the meaning:

The Natural State has no size. It is not bigger or smaller, longer or shorter; there is nothing at all which can be measured. This Nature is called the Perfected One. It cannot be described as 'purity' or 'knowledge' or 'fault' – you cannot say anything. Nature itself is the Perfected One. Whatever faults, purities or impurities arise simply appear as visions and they cannot alter or affect the Nature. Everything is allowed to come from this Nature. That is called 'perfected in Nature.'

There are two kinds of Perfection: Nature-Perfection and temporary perfection. Nature-Perfection refers to any visions which come when you practise and use the methods of Thögal. When thoughts appear, however, or anything which is connected with thoughts or perception, those are all temporary perfection or 'perfect as visions.' They come from the Nature but they are not Nature-Vision or Nature-Perfection. They are only temporarily perfected by consciousness and perception. If, on the other hand, visions are realized or permeated by the Wisdom Awareness, this is clear to you while you abide in the Nature, so if any emotions arise from the Nature, you can 'see' and 'control' them, so they will never lead you away from your Nature. They can come, and they all look like illusions. They come from the Nature into the Nature and you neither follow nor stop them. It is said here that they are all controlled by the King of Self-Awareness Wisdom.

That is the teaching.

Gyerza Dragchentsal

20. Namkha Nyima Wödenma

Namkha Nyima Wödenma transmitted the teachings to Nyima Tongkhyabma.

The symbol is the three miraculous mirrors one after the other.

The meaning is as follows:

When you look back towards a thought, nothing remains – no trace, nothing. Leave it as it is. Don't think anything about what happens after thoughts disappear. Remaining in this way is called 'keeping the Presence of Emptiness.' But if you are thinking that this Nature is empty, that means you are kept in the prison of emptiness.

If, instead of liberating your thought completely and allowing it to disappear, you are still thinking something; however subtle, such as: 'Nature is like this' or 'Nature is like that'; then this is like being unable to purify some sickness which you have inside your heart or some other inner organ. That is the example. You can discover this through the Shining Sun of Wisdom. No thoughts can disturb Wisdom, so no matter what kind of thoughts arise, just leave them. Don't follow them, don't try to stop them. If you don't do this, they will disturb your wisdom.

Don't think that followers of Dzogchen count the Ten Bhumis and the Five Paths, trying to climb up to Buddhahood using this system. If you do this, your Awareness Wisdom will set like the setting sun.

All kinds of emotions and defilements come, stay a while and disappear, and so they are something like a helper for recognizing the Nature. If you think that they are disturbances and judge them as something not good, then that means you have to follow evil again, that you have fallen down from the very narrow path.

In other words, you shouldn't try to recognize any kind of emotions or thoughts which arise. Just let them come. Don't follow them, don't try to stop them, nothing. You yourself try to remain as stably as possible in the Nature.

Namkha Nyima Wödenma

21. Nyima Tongkhyabma

Nyima Tongkhyabma transmitted the teachings to Khandro Mahasukasidtima. The symbol she showed is just remaining in the position of equipoise, the five-pointed posture.

The meaning and the teaching are as follows:

If you realize the Natural State clearly and know it perfectly well, then you have to practise, concentrate and meditate deeply; you have to become familiar with this State. Otherwise, if you merely think and decide: 'the Nature is this' or 'the Nature is that,' you are like a homeless man who doesn't belong anywhere. If you grasp at the Nature thinking 'this is right' or 'this is wrong' and making conceptual judgements, then that is not the right view.

The second thing is that you always have to try to remain purely and clearly in the Nature. Don't mix it with any thoughts. It doesn't matter whether they are rough thoughts like agitation or very subtle ones; either way, one day you are pretending to meditate, you think you are practising in a good way, but in fact you are not remaining in the real, essential Natural State properly. That is like the child you are fond of wandering off to the enemy. That is the example. You think you are practising meditation in a wonderful way but in fact you do not know the Nature in the proper way. It is quite important to first of all know what you are doing and then secondly to practise.

Then as for the meditation itself, always try to abide in the pure Nature. Otherwise it is difficult to make corrections. Nobody can tell you whether your view is right or wrong; it is up to you, the practitioner, to know this properly. So here it says that meditation is like a watchman, always keeping watch properly.

There are two aspects to the watchman in meditation. One is a kind of memory, Drenpa, another is Shezhin which means knowing,[72] and they are linked with consciousness. These two don't realize the Natural State but they know when you deviate from it. The remembering, Drenpa, knows whether you are in the right Nature or not. These two kinds of 'thought' are very important. The other one, Shezhin, can see and judge whether your Nature is right or wrong. Although it can see and judge this, it doesn't see the Nature itself. So it is quite interesting. This does not just apply to Dzogchen meditation. You need these two for any kind of meditation: remembering, Drenpa, and Shezhin, the

[72] Tib. dran pa, shes bzhin.

knower or knowing. We use a parable for these two and say they are like a shepherd. He keeps all the sheep inside the pen and so when he comes he doesn't need to take care of them, he can have a very good sleep. But if a sheep comes out then he is busy, you see, he is responsible for putting it back into the pen. So that is similar. Judging whether your meditation is right or wrong is remembering, Drenpa; it is one thought. While the sheep are kept in the pen he doesn't see them, but if a sheep comes out then he can see it. So in a similar way, Drenpa means remembering. As for the second one, if you are deluded or if your meditation is not going properly, it can see whether it is going the wrong way or not. This is Shezhin which knows that it is not right and puts it back. These two things are like a watchman keeping watch.

Nyima Tongkhyabma

The meditator has to try to be stable. It is useless to call yourself a 'yogi' if your meditation is not stable. When you come to the second stage,[73] you will have to go to the Bardo[74] like any ordinary person. That is the teaching on meditation or Gompa.[75]

Chyodpa[76] means activities. Always try to integrate your activities with the Natural State or with your realization of the Nature and then you will be able to control agitation. Agitation will no longer be rough or free to disturb you. In other words, it is controlled by your meditation. If your meditation cannot control agitation then even though you may be called a meditator, your practice and realization are just like those of a normal person.

That is the teaching.

22.Khandro Mahasukasidtima

Khandro Mahasukasidtima transmitted to Khandro Chöza Bönchigma.[77]

The symbol she showed is like this, just keeping in the normal five-pointed posture and holding her elbows with her two hands. That is the sign.

The teachings which Mahasukasidtima gave to Chöza Bönmo are the last in this lineage of Dakinis, but in fact Chöza Bönmo received the full Dzogchen teachings from Drenpa Namkha who compiled this text. She also received teachings from Lishu Tagring,[78] and Tonggyung Tuchen[79] – many Siddhas taught her. She was a very important lineage holder who kept many lineages, and preserved many texts during the time of persecution.

The teachings say:

The Natural State has no past, no future and no present. It is always the same. Therefore it is beyond time, and as such it is connected with all the Buddhas of the past, present and future. Moreover, it is imbued with Immeasurable Compassion which is already perfected within it, and as such it is connected with all sentient beings. This Nature has no source whatsoever; you cannot find its source using

---

[73] I.e. death.

[74] Tib. bar do.

[75] Tib. sgom pa.

[76] Tib. spyod pa.

[77] The root text gives Khandro Chöza Bönchigma (Tib. mKha' 'gro Co za Bon gcig ma) as her full name.

[78] Tib. Li shu sTag ring.

[79] Tib. sTong rgyung mThu chen.

perception. Where is the Nature? What happens in the Nature? You cannot explain anything or form any concepts. Then finally, this Natural State doesn't retain any traces whatsoever, yet all kinds of results and fruits are perfected within it, and as such, all phenomenal existence is integrated with Empty Form, or is liberated to Wisdom Awareness. Therefore there is nothing particular to practise such as Sutra or Tantra, yet the complete result of Buddhahood is easily found by a practitioner of Dzogchen.

That is the teaching.

Khandro Mahasukasidtima

23. Chöza Bönmo

Chöza Bönmo is the twenty-second lineage holder. Like the twenty-four Masters of the *Zhang Zhung Nyengyud*,[80] the Khandro of this lineage each received teachings, practised and achieved Rainbow Body, one after the other. Although the lineage continues after Chöza Bönmo, subsequent teachings are not recorded as not all the subsequent Khandro achieved Rainbow Body. They all received the teachings and practised, but not all of them practised successfully. The names of the women who received the teachings after Chöza Bönmo are listed here but not their teachings. So for example there is Gyagom Wöchamma,[81] who may have been from Gya or China, and Kyegom Chamme,[82] and Gommo Nyima.[83]

Chöza Bönmo composed and preserved many Dzogchen teachings during this critical time in the eighth century, so she was very helpful in preserving the Dzogchen lineages. Although she is twenty-second in the lineage, there are thirty teachings here, and the remaining ones were all taught by Chöza Bönmo; there is no successor. People were listening, practitioners were there, but they did not succeed in attaining Rainbow Body.

First of all, there are two Buddhas in this lineage, Satrig Ersang and Yiwongma, then the twenty-two Khandro, so there are twenty-four altogether – two Buddhas and the rest are human beings. There are many things in this text, including Dakini *sadhanas*,[84] so if someone is interested in practising Khandro Yoga instead of Guru Yoga, it is the same thing. 'Guru' means 'teacher' and a Khandro can be a teacher, too. So try hard to belong to this lineage of realized Khandro, so that a Westerner can join them.

Chöza Bönmo practised Guru Yoga and was able to invite the Gurus to come directly to the places she was staying and manifest visibly. That is the symbol which shows the power of Guru Yoga. That is the symbol she shows.

The teaching is:

There is no cause or support for the Natural State. It has neither

---

[80] Tib. *Zhang zhung snyan rguyd.*

[81] Tib. rGya sgom 'Od lcam ma.

[82] Tib. sKyed sgom lCam med.

[83] Tib. sGom mo Nyi ma. The names of these three Khandro were noted down from the recording by Geshe Namdak Nyima in Oxford, 24.12.2009.

[84] Tib sgrub pa.

beginning nor end. If you turn your consciousness towards the Nature, there is nothing special to see or hear, nor is it possible to explain where it resides. This Nature is called unchangeable Dharmakaya. There are no Paths, no Bhumis, nothing. Everything – the whole of phenomenal existence – is integrated with Awareness Wisdom. Everything is liberated there. If you don't realize this Nature purely yet expect to achieve the Three Kayas, there is no hope of receiving any result.

That is the teaching of the twenty-third session.

Chöza Bönmo

24.
The sign is showing Phowa with white A.

'Phowa' means integrating your own consciousness with the Natural State and we use the letter A for this practice as it represents consciousness. That is real, final Phowa but it is explained through the symbol Akar Phowa.[85]

As for the teaching itself:

Self-Originated Wisdom does not depend on either the Five Paths or the Ten Bhumis, nor does it rely on cause or fruit. The Nature encompasses the whole of existence equally, as space does, but nothing whatsoever can disturb it. The Nature itself is self-liberated. That is called the "Result which does not rely on anything else."

That is the teaching.

25.
The twenty-fifth session shows the sign of how Chöza Bönmo practised Guru Yoga.

As for the teaching or meaning:

Self-Originated Awareness Wisdom does not depend on cause or secondary cause. It cannot be destroyed, it does not die, nor can it exist as cause or fruit. Therefore this Nature cannot be measured according to the Ten Bhumis and Five Paths, nor is there any schedule as to when you achieve the Final Goal once you have received teachings. As for the seventeen different thoughts or understandings,[86] if you focus on the Nature, you are using thought, and thought is connected with perception, so that is the wrong way. It is better to look back towards the thought and let it liberate back into the Nature – that is the Final Goal and the Nature is seen clearly.

That is the twenty-fifth session.

26.
The twenty-sixth symbol shows how Chöza Bönmo visualized the six chakras clearly.

---

[85] Tib. a dkar 'pho ba.
[86] See translation of the root-text, p. 123, Footnote 12.

The twenty-sixth teaching is:

The Natural State appears spontaneously as Wisdom. There is no special cause or technique associated with this, for Wisdom is integrated with the Nature: Nature itself is Wisdom, Wisdom is Nature; there is no separation. Thus it is said: 'cause and fruit are equally perfected with Nature and Wisdom Awareness.' The Nine Ways and all other views are liberated into this Nature; whether someone realizes it or not, it encompasses all views. Faults and knowledge are also integrated with Awareness and Wisdom, appearing from there and liberating back there. All kinds of visions arise spontaneously, stay a while, and disappear, so they are empty, none other than Nature itself. This all happens by itself, there is nothing to be done. If you do something then you are deviating from the Nature. Everything is liberated back into the Nature.

That is the teaching.

27.
The symbol is to introduce the Natural State by using a mirror.

This is a good example as everyone has had the experience of looking into a mirror and seeing reflections. The meaning of this symbol is that you can see colours, forms and movements when you look in a mirror, but even though everything looks alive and moves, the mirror itself doesn't change or move. The mirror is like the Natural State and all kinds of visions appear spontaneously like reflections. Reflections are never separate from the mirror, so although you can always see things in a mirror – even things which are far away – those reflections can never be separated from the mirror itself. In the same way, all phenomena are integrated with the Natural State, and can never be separated from it. So this is a good example. You can remember it.

As for the teaching itself:

The Natural State is an unspeakable state. It is not possible to explain how it starts, how it arises, where it is, what the cause is, what its support is – we cannot explain anything. Also, it is not possible to explain which is right or wrong, what is clear and so on. Everything is created by words but words cannot clearly describe the Nature. All kinds of signs and material things are integrated with it, yet it is completely beyond anything material. All phenomena –

sounds, names, everything – are integrated with this Nature which is itself the View, Base, Path and Fruit of Dzogchen.

That is the teaching.

28.
The symbol is like practising Chöd,[87] offering the body to the Four Guests.

The Four Guests are:[88] the High Buddhas; the Highest Guardians; the Demi-gods;[89] normal sentient beings. Many demons belong to the class of Demi-gods. The fourth group is the normal sentient beings who expect to receive something from you. Chöd practitioners visualize that all these Guests receive something. The Buddhas don't expect to receive anything, so whatever you offer is for your own benefit. Then secondly we make offerings to the High Guardians and ask them to guard the doctrines and religion. The powerful Demi-gods can help if they are happy or like you, but they can be very dangerous if there is something wrong. So thirdly we make offerings to appease them, and this is like paying fees to those to whom we owe karmic debts. The fourth offering is like helping; we give these beings whatever they need.

There are four kinds of offering: Sang[90] in the morning; water offering at noon;[91] Sur[92] in the afternoon, and Chöd in the evening. These are all external supports or symbols, but when we do any of these practices, we think that we are offering dead people and normal spirits whatever they need. It is very important to think of this, especially for the dead. Spirits and the deceased are no longer connected with a material body or anything visible, so they are purely spirit or mind. The living are only connected to such beings through thinking, visualizing or remembering because these are movements of our consciousness, our mind. We can also have connection to the dead when we are asleep and dreaming. Although you are still linked with your material body when you sleep, the connection is not deep; your body is lying in bed but your mind is a little bit independent, thinking. That is a dream, and that is the only chance to meet with those who have lost their material body or have died. They come, and they can have some connection with

---

[87] Tib. gcod.
[88] Tib. mgron po bzhi.
[89] Tib. lha min.
[90] Tib. bsang.
[91] Tib. chu gtor.
[92] Tib. bsur.

living people. Don't think it is something bad if dead people come in dreams. Don't push them away. Quite a lot of people worry if they have dreams like this, and although some texts do explain that this is a bad sign or something, they are not all bad, not at all. The living and the dead are connected by desire or attachment and their only chance of meeting is in the dreamtime because the rest of the time we are deeply integrated with our material body, so it is not possible to see each other. If you dream of dead people or spirits, try to think about helping them, and these four offerings are a very great way to do that. The offering itself is just a symbol, a support; the main thing is to think you are helping sentient beings.[93]

The teaching is:

When you look back towards your thoughts, they liberate without a trace. There is no colour, no form, nothing which you can explain. This is called Empty Nature. But if you compare this Emptiness with that of the Madhyamaka or Chittamatra[94] View or with anything else and think that there are similarities, then you are making a mistake and deviating from the correct view. Dzogchen Nature is not connected with expectations, conceptual understanding or comparisons. It is completely beyond all this. Nor is it concerned with activities. So it cannot be compared with any other view, with any other view on emptiness. This Nature is only a vast unspeakable state, Great Bliss.

That is the teaching.

29.

The symbol for the twenty-ninth session is the Lion Posture. Place your two hands flat on the ground, and put your weight on the balls of your feet. The upper part of the body is raised, the head is up and the gaze is directed into space. Your knees don't touch the ground.

As for the teaching itself:

Yeshe Nampar Dagpa[95] – Pure Wisdom Awareness – is beyond any consciousness or perception, therefore there is not even the name

---

[93] For more details on Four Offerings see Ermakov, *Bө and Bön*, pp. 442-489.

[94] Tib. sems tsam pa.

[95] Tib. ye shes rnam par dag pa.

of Samsara, suffering or misery. None of the five aggregations is to be avoided as they simply liberate back into the Nature. That is called Nature-Buddha or Dharmakaya. This Nature is clear and aware of itself. All kinds of visions arise, but no matter what comes, they don't disturb it nor does it disturb the visions. They are called 'decorations of the Nature.' So this is Dharmakaya without sides, impartial Dharmakaya.

That is the teaching.

30.
The thirtieth symbol is like space. The whole universe is encompassed by empty space. This is the sign that this Nature is all-encompassing.

As for the teaching, this last, thirtieth teaching is like a piece of advice:

Any human being must try to be devoted to the Nature of Mind which is the Dzogchen View. If you do not have the good fortune to meet with these teachings, then no matter what else you do – either in terms of religion or in terms of normal activities – there is no hope of reaching the Final Goal. The text gives an example: when you want to milk a cow and go to milk the horn, you can't get anything! Or when a dog wants to lick something, it won't get anything if it licks space. So if you don't have any devotion to this State or Dzogchen, then whatever you do to purify your karma is just like washing or cleaning but being unable to beautify yourself; you are just missing the point. If you persist in following these activities you will become a Raksha[96] or an evil being. If you don't try to be devoted to this Nature or Dzogchen, it is like mixing good food with poison. This Nature is the real heart of beings. Don't miss this point by mentally grasping at views, meditation, activities or result; everything will go amiss if you don't follow this teaching, and if you miss this fundamental point you are ready to go to Samsara. Don't break this Samaya. If you do, there are very strict Guardians who are watching you. [97]

[96] Tib. srin po - an evil spirit.

[97] Yongdzin Rinpoche kindly clarified this point as follows: The first point of Dzogchen Samaya is that one must have a correct understanding of the Dzogchen View; secondly, one cannot simply make up one's own mind and form one's own opinion of the Nature of Mind according to one's own wishes; thirdly, one must not fall into mistaken understandings of the Dzogchen View, in particular, nihilism or eternalism. It is easy

Here the text gives the history of how this teaching survived. Drenpa Namkha compiled all the teachings of the Dakinis. First of all it was written in blue ink on copper sheeting. This text has been successively transmitted from one Dakini to another. In the eighth century the king and ministers were all foolish people and converted from Yungdrung Bön to Buddhism instead of living properly in keeping with the knowledge of the Nature. That means that those days were a time of persecution and all these precious teachings had to be hidden under rocks. These very essential teachings which are very precious, like gold, were not hidden among rocks or elsewhere but were kept in the mind or heart of the lineage-holders. These teachings were transmitted from one qualified person to another. It is not very common. Do not break your Samaya. You must be careful, it says.

---

to be mistaken, and this is very bad. Fourthly, one must respect anyone who has clearly understood the Dzogchen Nature. Any true Dzogchen practitioner should understand and respect the Dzogchen View, respect practitioners and spend time practising. These are the specific samaya relating to Dzogchen, but all Sutric and Tantric Samayas are included in this, as these doctrines were taught by the Buddha and one must not go against the Buddhas' teachings.

སྤྱི་རྒྱུད་ཆེན་མོ་ནམ་མཁའ་དཀར་པོ་ཡེ་ཁྲི་མཐའ་སེལ་ལས་
ཕོ་བརྒྱུད་དང་མོ་བརྒྱུད་གཉིས་ཀྱི་དོན་གྱི་གདམས་སྐོར་ལས་
མོ་བརྒྱུད་བརྡ་དོན་སུམ་ཅུ་པ་བཞུགས་སོ།།

ཅ༽ ༼ལྔ་པའོ།༽ ཡེ་ཤེས་མཁའ་འགྲོ་རིགས་ལྔའི་གཙོ་ལ་ཕྱག་འཚལ་ལོ། མོ་བརྒྱུད་བྱིན་རླབས་ཀྱི་གདམས་པ་འདི། ཡུམ་ས་ཏྲིག་ཨེར་སངས་དེ། དམ་ཚིག་གི་མཁའ་འགྲོ་མཛེས་མ་ཡིད་འོང་མར་སྐུ་སྤྲུལ་ནས། སྣང་སྲིད་དཔལ་མོ་དང་མཁའ་འགྲོ་གསལ་བར་མཛད་ནས། མོ་བརྒྱུད་ཐམས་ཅད་དབུགས་ཕྱུང་བ་ནི། ཟངས་ཀྱི་ཐང་ཤོག་ལ་མཐིང་གི་ཡི་གེ་བྲིས་པ་ཞིག བྱིན་གྱིས་རླབས་ཀྱིས་བར་སྣང་ཁམས་ནས་བླངས་ནས་གནང་ངོ་།།

དེ་རྒྱ་གར་གྱི་མཁའ་འགྲོ་མ་ཇུ་ལི་ཤག་གྱིས། སང་ཧི་ཏའི་སྐད་དུ་རང་གིས་རང་བསྒྱུར་རོ། འདི་ལ་དོན་རྣམ་པ་གཉིས་ཏེ། བརྡ་དམར་ཁྲིད་དུ་བསྟན་པ་དང་། དོན་རིག་པ་སེམས་ཐོག་ཏུ་དབབ་པའོ།།

དམ་ཚིག་གི་མཁའ་འགྲོས། རྒྱ་གར་གྱི་མཁའ་འགྲོ་མ་ལ། ཀ༽ བརྡ་དང་པོ་བར་སྣང་འོད་ཀྱི་ཐག་པའི་བརྡ་བསྟན། ཀ༽ དོན་དང་པོ་ཡེ་ནས་བྱང་སེམས་བོན་སྐུ་འདི། ཕུང་ལྔ་ལས་སོགས་མེད་པས་དར་ཞིང་རྒུད་པ་མེད། སྐྱེ་འཆི་འདུ་འབྲལ་མེད་པས་གསང་གཅད་ཡུལ་མ་གྲུབ། སྣང་སྲིད་སེམས་སུ་འདུས་ཤིང་ཡེ་ནས་བོན་སྐུར་གནས། ཞེས་གསུངས་སོ། །དེས་རིག་འཛིན་རིག་པས་བརྒྱུད་དེ། ཟག་བཅས་ལྔ་ལ་བརྒྱུད་དོ།།

THIRTY SIGNS AND MEANINGS OF THE FEMALE LINEAGE

from The Cycle of Essential Instructions of the Male and Female Lineages, from The Great General Tantra, White Sky: Liberating Extremes of the Mind

Homage to the principal wisdom Khandro of the five Buddha families!

This is the blessed instruction of the female lineage.

The mother, Satrig Ersang, emanated as the Damtsig Khandro[1] Dzema Yiwongma. Having transformed all the visions of existence into Walmo and Khandro, Dzema Yiwongma released all the suffering of all female beings. Through the power of blessings, she plucked these teachings written in lapis lazuli ink on a copper sheet from space and gave them to the Khandro Ulishak.

Ulishak, the Khandro from India, translated them into Sanskrit herself. This teaching comprises two principle aspects: firstly, the quintessential instructions taught through symbols; and secondly, the explanation by which the direct meaning of awareness is settled in the mind.

1. Damtsig Khandro (Dzema Yiwongma) showed the first symbol to the Indian Khandro Ulishak, the sign of a rope of light in space.

As for the first meaning:

This primordial Bönku[2] of Bodhichitta is free from the five aggregates. It knows neither youth nor old age, neither increase nor decrease. Since it is beyond birth and death, it is beyond amalgamation and disintegration. Thus it has never been something which can be destroyed. All appearances and whatever exists are within the Mind and abide in the dimension of primordial Bönku.

Thus she spoke.

From there, the mind lineage of the Rigdzins[3] was transmitted to

[1] The Khandro of Spiritual Pledge.
[2] Tib. bon sku. Skt. dharmakaya - Body of Ultimate Reality.
[3] The Holders of Primordial Awareness.

རྒྱ་གར་མཁའ་འགྲོ་ཨུ་ཡི་ཤག་གིས། དཔལ་མོ་ཟ་ནམ་མཁའ་འོད་ཀྱི་རྒྱལ་མོ་ལ།
ཀ༽ བརྡ་གཉིས་པ་ཐལ་ལོ་གནམ་བརྫོལ་གྱི་བརྡ་བསྟན། ཁ ༽ དོན་གཉིས་པ་མི་
ནུབ་རྒྱལ་མཚན་བྱང་ཆུབ་སེམས་ཉིད་ལ། མཐར་ཐུག་མེད་ཕྱིར་བོན་སྐུ་བྲི་གང་མེད།
འགྱུར་བ་མེད་པས་དུས་གསུམ་གཡུང་དྲུང་ཆེ། འཁོར་འདས་གཞི་རྩ་མི་སྲོང་ཡེ་ནས་
རྒྱལ་མཚན་དང་། ཞེས་གསུངས་སོ།།

དཔལ་མོ་ཟས་རྣ་ཞགས་ཟ་གསལ་བ་དབྱིངས་ཕྱུག་མ་ལ། ག ༽ བརྡ་གསུམ་པ་རང་
ལུས་གནམ་འགྲིང་གི་བརྡ་བསྟན། ག༽ དོན་གསུམ་པ་སེམས་ཀྱི་མཚན་ཉིད་ཡེ་
སངས་རྒྱས་པའི་ངང་། རྒྱུ་རྐྱེན་རྟོག་བྲལ་གཡུང་དྲུང་བྱང་ཆུབ་སེམས། ལུས་སེམས་
མི་བཙོས་ཡན་པ་བོན་ཉིད་ཀློང་། སྣང་སྟོང་མཐའ་བྲལ་གདོད་ནས་རང་བྱུང་སྐུ།
ཞེས་གསུངས་སོ།།

རྣ་ཞགས་ཟས་ཞང་ཞུང་ཟ་འོད་ཀྱི་བླ་མ་ལ། ང ༽ བརྡ་བཞི་པ་ཕྱག་མཇུབ་ལྟག་
འཐེན་གྱི་བརྡ་བསྟན། ང༽ དོན་བཞི་པ་ཡེ་ནས་མ་བསྒྲིབས་སེམས་ཉིད་སྟོང་གསལ་
དང་། སེམས་ལ་སེམས་བལྟས་སྣང་བའི་དངོས་པོ་ཟད། བལྟར་མེད་གཟུང་ཡུལ་
མཐའ་ལས་འདས་པར་བཞག དེ་ཉིད་སེམས་ཀྱི་ཀློང་སྟེ་བསྒོམ་ཡུལ་རིག་པར་གྲོལ།
ཞེས་གསུངས་སོ།།

the lineage of gods.[4]

2. The Khandro from India, Ulishak, showed the second symbol to Walmoza Namkha Wökyi Gyalmo, the sign of palms suddenly manifesting in space.

As for the second meaning:

The Nature of pure and perfect Mind is like a victory banner which is never furled. Since it is absolute, Bönku knows neither increase nor decrease. This is the great Swastika which remains immutable throughout the three times. This is the pristine banner of victory which is primordially free from the extremes of Samsara or Nirvana yet rejects the base of neither.

Thus she spoke.

3. Walmoza showed the third symbol to Razhagza Salwa Yingchyugma, the sign of standing in space.

As for the third meaning:

The quality of the Nature of primordial Buddhahood is unborn and unobstructed pure and perfect mind which is free from primary causes, secondary causes and discursive thoughts. Leave body and mind free and uncorrected in the dimension of Bönnyi,[5] the Natural State. This is the primordial, self-originated body, Rangjyung Ku,[6] free from the extremes of appearances and emptiness.

Thus she spoke.

4. Razhagza showed the fourth symbol to Zhangzhungza Wökyi Lama, the sign of hooking her two index fingers at the back of her head.

As for the fourth meaning:

The empty, clear Nature of Mind is naturally unobscured. When the mind looks to the mind, all appearances are exhausted. Settle in a state where there is nothing to be viewed as either subject or object. This is the dimension of the Nature of Mind in which the object of meditation is liberated into intrinsic awareness.

Thus she spoke.

[4] The lineage here is the human one.
[5] Tib. bon nyid - Ultimate Nature of Reality.
[6] Tib. rang byung sku.

ཞང་ཞུང་ཟས་ལྡོང་ལྷམ་འཕར་མོ་སྐྱོང་ལ། ཙ ༽ བརྡ་ལྔ་པ་འགྱུ་བ་རང་འགགས་ཀྱི་བརྡ་བསྟན། ཙ ༽ དོན་ལྔ་པ་སེམས་ཀྱི་དཔེ་ནི་ནམ་མཁའ་དོན་ནི་ཡེ་སངས་རྒྱས། སྟོང་གསལ་འདུས་མ་བྱས་པས་རིག་པ་མཐའ་དབུས་བདལ། མཚན་མའི་ཡུལ་ལས་འདས་པས་སྟོང་པ་བོན་གྱི་སྐུ། ཅིར་སྣང་སྟེང་དུ་རིག་པ་དྲིལ་ལ་བཞག ཅེས་གསུངས་སོ།།

ལྡོང་ལྷམ་གྱིས་སྟག་གསིག་ཟ་མང་བྱེད་གསལ་བྱེད་འོད་ལ། ཚ༽ བརྡ་དྲུག་པ་བར་སྣང་འོད་ཀྱི་བརྡ་བསྟན། ཚ ༽ དོན་དྲུག་པ་སེམས་ཉིད་བརྟགས་པས་ཅིར་སྣང་ཀ་ནས་དག རང་སྣང་གྲོལ་བས་གཉིས་མེད་བོན་གྱི་སྐུ། སྣང་སྲིད་ཀུན་གྲོལ་མ་སྤངས་སངས་རྒྱས་རྗེ། ཆོ་འཕྲུལ་ཅིར་སྣང་རིག་པའི་རྩལ་དུ་གྲུབ། ཅེས་གསུངས་སོ།།

སྟག་གཟིག་ཟས་ཨཱ་རྒྱན་ཟ་རིགས་ངན་བདུད་རྩི་སྐྱོང་ལ། ཛ ༽ བརྡ་བདུན་པ་ལག་ཞགས་བརྒྱ་འཕྲུད་ཀྱི་བརྡ་བསྟན། ཛ ༽ དོན་བདུན་པ་སེམས་ཉིད་ཡེ་ནས་སྟོང་བདལ་ནམ་མཁའ་ལ། ཕྱག་རྒྱའི་དཀྱིལ་འཁོར་གཟུགས་དང་ཁ་དོག་འབྱུང་། སེམས་ཀྱི་བོན་ཉིད་དོན་ལས་གཡོས་པ་མེད། མ་གཡོས་ངང་ལ་གནས་པ་བོན་ཉིད་རྒྱ། ཞེས་གསུངས་སོ།།

5. Zhangzhungza showed the fifth symbol to Dongcham Kharmokyong, the sign of the spontaneous cessation of discursive thoughts.

As for the fifth meaning:

As for the Natural State, the example is the sky, and the meaning is primordial Buddhahood. Everything is equally pervaded by intrinsic awareness which is empty, clear, and unconditioned. The empty Nature of Mind is beyond the dualism of subject and object. No matter what appearances arise, settle and integrate them into intrinsic awareness.

Thus she spoke.

6. Dongcham showed the sixth symbol to Tagzigza Manggye Salgyewö, the sign of light in space.

As for the sixth meaning:

Even if we analyze the Nature of Mind, we realize that whatever appears is primordially pure. Self-manifesting liberation is non-dual Bönku. All appearances and whatever exists are liberated; nothing is rejected. That is supreme Buddhahood. Any visions which manifest are but reflections of intrinsic awareness.

Thus she spoke.

7. Tagzigza showed Urgyenza Rigden Düdtsikyong the seventh sign, the symbol of holding her hands under her thighs.

As for the seventh meaning:

The Nature of Mind is primordially empty and omni-pervasive, like space. All the mandalas, forms and hues of the divinities emerge from this Nature, yet the essence of the Nature of Mind remains unperturbed. Abiding in this imperturbable Nature is the seal of the Natural State.

Thus she spoke.

ཨུ་རྒྱན་མས་རྒྱ་གར་ཕ་མཐིང་ཟ་མཐུ་ཆེན་ལ། ཉ༽ བརྡ་བརྒྱད་པ་གཞོགས་བསྙེངས་ལག་མནན་གྱི་བརྡ་བསྟན། ཉ༽ དོན་བརྒྱད་པ་སེམས་ཉིད་དམིགས་སུ་མེད་པས་བོན་སྐུ་རྩོལ་ལས་འདས། ཁ་དོག་དབྱིངས་དང་བོངས་ཚད་ཡུལ་དང་བྲལ། གདོད་ནས་སྐྱེ་འཛིགས་མེད་པས་གཉེན་པོས་གཞོམ་དུ་མེད། དམིགས་མེད་སྟོང་བདལ་ནམ་མཁའི་ངང་དུ་གནས། ཞེས་གསུངས་སོ།།

ཕ་མཐིང་ཟས་རྒྱ་ཟ་གསལ་བ་འོད་སྒྲོན་ལ། ཏ༽ བརྡ་དགུ་པ་ཡི་དམ་ཁྲོ་ལ་འཕོ་བར་བསྟན། ཏ༽ དོན་དགུ་པ་སྣང་སྲིད་རིག་པར་ཤར་བས་ཉི་ཟླ་སྟོང་བས་ལྷག གསལ་ཁྱབ་ཆེན་པོར་གནས་པས་མ་རིག་མུན་པ་སེལ། ཡི་ནས་སངས་རྒྱས་ཡིན་པས་འཁོར་བ་དོང་ནས་སྤྲུགས། སྔ་ཕྱི་ཐ་དད་མེད་པས་དུས་གསུམ་གཅིག་ཏུ་འདྲིལ། ཞེས་གསུངས་སོ།།

རྒྱ་ཟ་གསལ་བས་གཡོར་པོ་ཟ་དྲི་མེད་མདངས་ལྡན་མ་ལ། ཐ༽ བརྡ་བཅུ་པ་སེམས་ཉིད་འོད་གསལ་གཞི་ལ་འཕོ་བའི་བརྡ་བསྟན། ཐ༽ དོན་བཅུ་པ་སེམས་ཉིད་བདུད་རྩི་ཆེན་པོའི་རང་བཞིན་ཏེ། ཕྱི་ནང་ཀུན་ལ་སྤྱོད་པས་གང་ཤར་བདུད་རྩི་ཡིན། ཅེར་སྣང་རྒྱ་ཡིས་ཐེབས་པས་རང་རིག་བདུད་རྩིའི་མཆོག རྒྱ་ཡན་གློང་དུ་བདལ་བས་བོན་སྐུ་བདུད་རྩི་གྲུབ། ཅེས་གསུངས་སོ།།

8. Urgyenza showed the eighth symbol to Gyagar Phamthingza Thuchenma, the sign of lying and pressing her hand.[7]

As for the eighth meaning:

Since the Nature of Mind is inconceivable, Bönku is beyond effort. This Nature is free from colour, shape, size and objects. Primordially unborn and indestructible, it cannot be liberated by any antidote. It abides naturally free from concepts, it is empty, and pervades everywhere equally, like the sky.

Thus she spoke.

9. Phamthingza showed the ninth symbol to Gyaza Salwa Wödronma, the sign of the transference[8] into the wrathful *yidam*.

As for the ninth meaning:

As all appearances and whatever exists arise within intrinsic awareness, their brightness surpasses that of a thousand suns and a thousand moons. When we remain in this great, pervasive clarity, the darkness of ignorance is cleared away. Since this state is primordial Buddhahood, Samsara is completely reversed. As there is no separation into past and future, the three times are essentialised as one in the Natural State.

Thus she spoke.

10. Gyaza showed the tenth symbol to Yorpoza Drime Dangdenma, the sign of transferring the clear light of the Natural State into the Base.

As for the tenth meaning:

The Natural State is like the essence of great *düdtsi*.[9] When you enjoy all external and internal phenomena of existence within the Natural State, whatever arises is *düdtsi*. Any phenomena or appearances which are sealed by the Natural State are the excellent *düdtsi* of self-awareness. By remaining carefree in the Natural

[7] See Yongdzin Rinpoche's commentary, p. 66.

[8] I.e. Tib. 'pho ba.

[9] This term is often translated as 'nectar.' In fact, it comprises two Tibetan words: bdud - demons, negativities; and rtsi – clearing away. Thus it is a substance which clears away or liberates all negativities. It is sometimes referred to as a medicine.

གཡོར་པོ་ཟླས་གཙོ་ཟླ་འོད་ཀྱི་རྫུ་འཕྲུལ་སྟོན་ལ། ད ༽ བརྡ་བཅུ་གཅིག་པ་ལག་གཡས་ལུས་བསྐུམས་གཙུད་པའི་བརྡ་བསྟན། ད ༽ དོན་བཅུ་གཅིག་པ་སེམས་ཀྱི་ཐོན་ཉིད་ནམ་མཁའ་འདྲ། ཡེ་ནས་སྟོང་བདག་མེད་པར་ཁྱབ། སེམས་ཀྱི་ཐོན་ཉིད་པད་མ་འདྲ། ཕྱི་ནང་སྐྱོན་ཡོན་མཐའ་དང་བྲལ། སེམས་ཀྱི་ཐོན་ཉིད་རིན་ཆེན་གཏེར། དགོས་འདོད་རིག་པ་སེམས་ལས་འབྱུང་། སེམས་ཀྱི་ཐོན་ཉིད་གཞའ་ཚོན་འདྲ། སྣང་སྟོང་གཉིས་མེད་ཐོན་གྱི་སྐུ། ཞེས་གསུངས་སོ།།

གཙོ་ཟླས་བྲུ་ཤ་ཟླ་རྫུ་འཕྲུལ་སྣ་ཚོགས་སྟོན་ལ། ན༽ བརྡ་བཅུ་གཉིས་པ་འོད་ཀྱི་འཁོར་ལོ་རྣམ་དྲུག་གི་བརྡ་བསྟན། ན༽ དོན་བཅུ་གཉིས་པ་ཐོན་ཉིད་སེམས་ཀྱི་གནས་ལུགས་འདི། དངོས་པོ་མཚན་མར་མ་གྲུབ་རྟག་མཐའ་བྲལ། ཕྲང་ཆད་ཉེ་ཚེར་མ་སོང་ཆད་པའི་མཐའ་དང་བྲལ། ཡུལ་དྲུག་ངེས་པར་མི་གཅོད་བདག་ཏུ་འཛིན་པ་བྲལ། ཕྱོགས་དང་ཁ་དོག་མ་གྲུབ་མཚན་མར་འཛིན་པ་གྲོལ། ཞེས་གསུངས་སོ།།

State, the *düdtsi* of Bönku is accomplished.

Thus she spoke.

11. Yorpoza showed the eleventh symbol to Chöza Wökyi Dzutrultön, the sign of bending her right hand and twisting her body.

As for the eleventh meaning:

The Nature of Mind is like the sky; it is primordially self-less and all-encompassing.
The Nature of Mind is like a lotus; it is free from the extremes of being flawed or correct, either externally or internally.
The Nature of Mind is like a precious jewel; whatever is needed or wished for originates from the mind of awareness.
The Nature of Mind is like a rainbow; the body of Dharmakaya, Bönku, is the non-duality of appearances and emptiness.

Thus she spoke.

12. Chöza showed the twelfth symbol to Drushaza Dzutrul Natsogtön, the sign of the six wheels of light.

As for the twelfth meaning:

The Natural State is the Nature of the Mind. Since it possesses neither inherent existence nor materiality, it is beyond the extreme of eternalism. Since it has never been either void or temporary, it is beyond the extreme of nihilism. Since it does not grasp at the six specific objects,[10] it is free from clinging to the concept of the self. Since it cannot be comprehended in terms of sides and colours, the grasper of ordinary attributes is liberated.

Thus she spoke.

---

[10] The objects of the six senses, i.e. the five senses plus the mind.

ཟླ་ཤ་ཟས་ལུང་རྒྱན་ཟ་སྣང་བ་བརྡ་སྟོན་མ་ལ། པ༽ བརྡ་བཅུ་གསུམ་པ་ཐབས་དང་ཤེས་རབ་འོད་སྦྲེལ་གྱི་བརྡ་བསྟན། པ༽ དོན་བཅུ་གསུམ་པ་འདུ་འབྲལ་གྲོལ་འགྲུལ་མེད་པས་རྟག་པ་ཆེན་པོའི་དང་། དངོས་འཛིན་ཡོད་རྟག་བྲལ་བས་ཆད་པ་ལྷུན་གྱིས་གྲུབ། སྣང་སྲིད་རང་རྒྱས་ཐེབས་པས་བདག་ཉིད་ཆེན་པོ་ཡིན། སྣང་སྲིད་རིག་པར་ཤར་བས་མཚན་མར་འཛིན་པ་ཡིན། ཞེས་གསུངས་སོ།།

ལུང་རྒྱན་ཟས་མེ་ཉག་ཟ་ཐོག་འབེབས་མ་ལ། ཕ༽ བརྡ་བཅུ་བཞི་པ་སེང་གེ་ཁྲི་ཚུགས་བར་སྣང་ལ་གཏད་པའི་བརྡ་བསྟན། ཕ༽ དོན་བཅུ་བཞི་པ་སྣང་བ་འོད་སྣང་མི་སྤྲང་རིག་པའི་རྩལ་དུ་ཤེས། འཛིན་རྟོག་གང་ཤར་རིག་པའི་རྩེ་ས་ཡིན། གང་ཤར་དེ་ལ་མི་རྟོག་རིག་པའི་གྲོལ་ས་ཡིན། གདོད་ནས་ཅིར་མི་དགོངས་པ་འབྲས་བུར་གྲོལ་བ་ཡིན། ཞེས་གསུངས་སོ།།

མེ་ཉག་ཟས་ཨཱ་རྒྱན་ཟ་ནམ་མཁའ་ལྡུམ་ལ། བ༽ བརྡ་བཅོ་ལྔ་པ་འོད་རིག་དབྱིངས་ནས་དྲང་བའི་བརྡ་བསྟན། བ༽ དོན་བཅོ་ལྔ་པ་སེམས་ཀྱི་བོན་ཉིད་མཚན་མའི་ཡུལ་ལས་འདས། མངོན་སུམ་མི་གནས་སྣང་སྲིད་ཀུན་ལ་ཁྱབ། ཐ་སྙད་མེད་པས་ཡེ་ཤེས་མིང་མ་གྲུབ། བསྟན་མེད་སྐྱེ་འཇིག་བྲལ་བས་གཡུང་དྲུང་ཕ་ལམ་འདྲ། ཞེས་གསུངས་སོ།།

13. Drushaza showed the thirteenth symbol to Lunggyenza Nangwa Datönma, the sign of combined light, the union of wisdom and method.

As for the thirteenth meaning:

This Nature is free from amalgamation and separation, liberation and delusion, thus it is called Great Eternalism.
It is free from the extremes of apprehended reality, existence and eternalism, thus it is called Spontaneously Perfected Nihilism.
All appearances and whatever exists are sealed by their self-nature, thus it is called the Great Self.
All appearances and whatever exists arise within intrinsic awareness, thus it is called the Grasper of Objects.

Thus she spoke.

14. Lunggyenza showed the fourteenth symbol to Menyagza Thogbebma, the sign of the lion position, gazing in space.

As for the fourteenth meaning:

When the visions of clear light are not renounced, the reflections of awareness are recognized. No matter what grasping or discursive thoughts arise, they are but the playground of intrinsic awareness.

When whatever arises is not conceptualized, that is the liberation ground of intrinsic awareness. Being primordially free from desire, it liberates into the final result.

Thus she spoke.

15. Menyagza showed the fifteenth symbol to Urgyenza Namkhacham, the sign of bringing light from the dimension of awareness.

As for the fifteenth meaning:

The Nature of Mind is beyond being the object of dualistic thought. It does not appear visibly yet it pervades all appearances and whatever exists. Since it is inexpressible, there is no name of primordial wisdom. Since it cannot be shown, created or destroyed, it is like an indestructible diamond swastika.

Thus she spoke.

ཨུ་རྒྱན་ཟས་ཤྲཱི་བེར་ཟ་འོད་ཐང་མ་ལ། མ༽ བརྡ་བཅུ་དྲུག་པ་ཐིག་ལེ་ལྷུ་གཅུད་ཀྱི་བརྡ་བསྟན། མ༽ དོན་བཅུ་དྲུག་པ་རིག་པ་སེམས་ལ་འདི་ཞེས་བསྟན་དུ་མེད། གཡུང་དྲུང་སེམས་ལ་ཚད་དཔག་མཚོན་དུ་མེད། རང་རིག་དོན་ལ་གདོད་ནས་འདུ་འབྲལ་མེད། བོན་སྐུ་སྣང་བ་རང་གྲོལ་སེམས་ལ་འདུད། ཅེས་གསུངས་སོ།།

ཤྲཱི་བེར་ཟས་ཁ་ཆེ་ཟ་རྒྱན་ལྡན་མ་ལ། ཙ༽ བརྡ་བཅུ་བདུན་པ་མནན་ལུས་བགས་བཅུའི་བརྡ་བསྟན། ཙ༽ དོན་བཅུ་བདུན་པ་གཡུང་དྲུང་སེམས་ཉིད་མཐའ་དབུས་བདལ་པས་ནམ་མཁའ་ཆེ། དོན་ལ་འགྱུར་བ་མེད་པས་གཡུང་དྲུང་ནམ་མཁའ་ཆེ། དགག་སྒྲུབ་བྱས་བཅོས་གྲོལ་བས་མི་དགོངས་ནམ་མཁའ་ཆེ། གང་ལྟར་སྤྱོད་པས་མི་ཟད་རིན་ཆེན་ནམ་མཁའ་ཆེ། ཞེས་གསུངས་སོ།།

ཁ་ཆེ་ཟས་གྱེར་ཟ་བྲག་ཆེན་རྩལ་ལ། ཚ༽ བརྡ་བཅོ་བརྒྱད་པ་མཉམ་བཞག་ཁྲིག་འཛིན་གྱི་བརྡ་བསྟན། ཚ༽ དོན་བཅོ་བརྒྱད་པ་བོན་ཉིད་ཕྱོགས་མེད་ནམ་མཁས་ཀུན་ཀ་མ་སྤྱངས་པས། ཉོན་མོངས་ལས་སོགས་སྒྲིབ་དང་ཁྲུ་རླངས་བྱུང་ཞིང་ཐིམ། རིག་པའི་ངང་ལས་མཚན་མ་ཅིར་ཤར་ཀྱང་། བོན་ཉིད་ཀློང་ལས་གར་ཡང་འདའ་བ་མེད། སྣང་སྲིད་རིག་པའི་ཀློང་དུ་ཤར་ཅིང་གྲོལ། བཟང་ངན་རྟོག་པར་མི་འབྱེད་རང་རིག་དབྱེ་བསལ་མེད། གསལ་འགྲིབ་མེད་པས་ཉིན་མཚན་ཟང་ཐལ་ཤར། ཅེས་གསུངས་སོ།།

16. Urgyenza showed the sixteenth symbol to Shiwerza Wöthangma, the sign of five thigles spinning in space.

As for the sixteenth meaning:

The mind of awareness cannot be shown concretely. The Nature of Mind cannot be conjectured, neither can it be shown through examples. The essence of self-awareness can naturally never be amalgamated or separated. Bönku and the self-liberation of visions are integrated in the Natural State.

Thus she spoke.

17. Shiwerza showed the seventeenth symbol to Khacheza Gyendenma, the sign of balancing all ten aspects of the body.

As for the seventeenth meaning:

The unborn, indestructible Nature of Mind pervades all things equally without centre or borders. It is like the vast sky. The essence is immutable, like the unborn, indestructible, boundless sky. The Nature of Mind liberates denying, affirming, fabrication, and modification. It is carefree like the boundless sky. No matter how many or how varied the manifestations you use and enjoy, this Nature is inexhaustible, like the precious treasury of the vast sky.

Thus she spoke.

18. Khacheza showed the eighteenth symbol to Gyerza Dragchentsal, the sign of drawing her hands into the well-arranged posture of equipoise.

As for the eighteenth meaning:

The Nature of Mind is free from partiality; like space, it rejects nothing. All defiling emotions and so forth arise from Nature and dissolve back into it, like clouds and mist which arise and dissolve in space. None of the myriad phenomena which arise from the Nature of Awareness ever go beyond the dimension of the Natural State. All appearances and whatever exists emerge from the dimension of intrinsic awareness and liberate into it. As everything is integrated within inseparable self-awareness, there is no distinction between good or bad thoughts. This Nature of Awareness neither brightens nor dims; it arises clearly without day and night.

Thus she spoke.

གྱེར་ཟབ་ནམ་མཁའ་ཉི་མ་འོད་ལྡན་མ་ལ། ༼ཛ༽ བརྡ་བཅུ་དགུ་པ་ཐལ་མོ་གཉིས་
དཀུ་མནན་གྱི་བརྡ་བསྟན། ༼ཛ༽ དོན་བཅུ་དགུ་པ་སེམས་ཉིད་བོངས་ཚད་མེད་
པས་ཆེ་ཆུང་ཡེ་ནས་གྲོལ། བོན་སྐུར་ལྷུན་གྱིས་གྲུབ་པས་སྐྱོན་ཡོན་རང་སར་དག
སྐྱོན་སྣང་གཞི་ནས་བཅོམ་པས་ཡོན་ཏན་ངང་གིས་རྫོགས། རིག་ཤེས་རྒྱལ་པོ་ཟིན་
པས་ཉོན་མོངས་ཆམ་ལ་ཕབ། ཞེས་གསུངས་སོ། །

ཉི་མ་འོད་ལྡན་མས་ཉི་མ་སྟོང་ཁྱབ་ལ། ཝ༽ བརྡ་ཉི་ཤུ་པ་འཕྲུལ་གྱི་མེ་ལོང་སུམ་
ཐུགས་ཀྱི་བརྡ་བསྟན། ཝ༽ དོན་ཉི་ཤུ་པ་སྟོང་པ་བཙོན་དུ་མ་བཟུང་མཚན་མའི་
ཕུར་པ་བཏབ། འཛིན་རྟོག་ཁོང་སྲན་མ་ཐོན་ཡེ་ཤེས་ཉི་མ་ནུབ། དྲན་རྟོག་ཡེ་ཤེས་
མ་བསླངས་ས་ལམ་འཛོགས་ཤིང་ནུབ། བདུད་སྣང་གྲོགས་སུ་མ་ཤར་ཉམས་ཀྱིས་
འཕྲང་ཤོར། ཞེས་གསུངས་སོ། །

མཁའ་འགྲོ་ཉི་མ་སྟོང་ཁྱབ་མས་མཁའ་འགྲོ་མ་ཏ་སུ་ག་སིད་ཏི་ལ། ཞ༽ བརྡ་ཉེར་
གཅིག་པ་མནན་ལུས་རིག་པ་རང་གདངས་ཀྱི་བརྡ་བསྟན། ཞ༽ དོན་ཉེར་གཅིག་པ་
དོན་གྱི་གདེང་གིས་མ་ཟིན་ན། འབད་རྩོལ་གྱི་བུ་མོ་གྲོང་ཁ་ཡན། ལྟ་བའི་སྲུང་མ་མི་
འགོ་ན། རང་སེམས་བུ་གཅེས་དགྲ་ལག་འཚོར། སྒོམ་པའི་སོ་སྲུང་མ་ཚུགས་ན། རྣལ་
འབྱོར་གྱི་མཚན་སྨན་གྱི་བར་དོར་འཕྲམས། སྤྱོད་པའི་སྤྲང་ཆེན་མ་ཐུལ་ན། གཤེན་
རབ་ཀྱི་ལྟ་བ་སྒྲི་སར་ལྟས། ཞེས་གསུངས་སོ། །

19. Gyerza showed the nineteenth symbol to Namkha Nyima Wödenma, the sign of pressing her two palms against her hips.

As for the nineteenth meaning:

The Nature of Mind is beyond measurements, thus it is primordially free from being large or small.

Since everything is spontaneously perfected in Bönku, faults and virtuous qualities liberate by themselves. Once all faults and delusions are cleared from the Base, all the qualities of Buddhahood are naturally achieved. Once the King of Awareness has been realized, all defilements are vanquished.

Thus she spoke.

20. Nyima Wödenma showed the twentieth symbol to Nyima Tongkhyabma, the sign of the mind, the three miraculous mirrors.

As for the twentieth meaning:

If you do not recognize Empty Nature, you are bound to the tethering post of dualistic vision.
If you cannot patiently bear grasping and discursive thoughts, the Sun of Primordial Wisdom will set.
If you yourself do not integrate your mind and discursive thoughts with Primordial Wisdom, you will climb along the Path and Bhumis and your Primordial Wisdom will wane.
If demonic visions do not arise as helpers for your practice, you will deviate into the path of error. Thus she spoke.

21. Khandro Nyima Tongkhyabma showed the twenty-first sign to Khandro Mahasukasitima, the sign of self-radiant awareness, the balanced body posture.

As for the twenty-first meaning:

If you do not maintain confidence in the Natural State, your struggles and efforts are like those of a homeless girl roaming wild. If you do not guard your view, it is like chasing the precious child of your own mind into the hands of the enemy.
If you are unable to remain in stable meditation, you are merely running after the reputation of being a great practitioner, and will wander in Bardo. If you do not tame the wild elephant of conduct, your view is just like that of an ordinary person.

Thus she spoke.

མཁའ་འགྲོ་མ་ཧ་སུ་ཀ་སིད་དྷི་ཡིས་མཁའ་འགྲོ་གཙོ་ཟ་བོན་ཅིག་ལ། ཟ༽ བརྡ་ཉེར་གཉིས་པ་ལག་འབྱུང་དོན་གསལ་གྱི་བརྡ་བསྟན། ཟ༽ དོན་ཉེར་གཉིས་པ་སེམས་ལ་ཕྱ་ཕྱི་མེད་པས་དུས་གསུམ་སངས་རྒྱས་ཀུན་དང་འབྲེལ། སྙིང་རྗེ་ཚད་མེད་སེམས་སུ་འདུས་པས་ཁམས་གསུམ་སེམས་ཅན་ཀུན་དང་འབྲེལ། བྱང་ས་གནས་ས་ཐིམ་པ་ཤེས་པས་ལམ་དང་འབྲས་བུ་ཀུན་དང་འབྲེལ། སྣང་སྟོང་རིག་པར་གྲོལ་བས་མ་བསྒྲུབས་འབྲས་བུ་རང་ལ་རྙེད། ཅེས་གསུངས་སོ། །

འ༽ །བརྡ་ཉེར་གསུམ་པ་ཟླ་མ་བཅུད་སྟུད་ཀྱི་བརྡ་བསྟན། འ༽ དོན་ཉེར་གསུམ་པ་རྒྱུ་རྐྱེན་གྱིས་མ་བསྐྱེད་པས་ཐོག་མར་སྐྱེ་བའི་གཞི་མེད། ངེས་མེད་ཆེན་པོར་འདུག་པས་བར་དུ་གནས་པའི་ཡུལ་མེད། བོན་གྱི་སྐུ་ལ་འགྱུར་བ་མེད་པས་ཐ་མར་འགྲོ་བའི་ལམ་མེད། སྣང་སྲིད་རིག་པའི་ཀློང་དུ་གྲོལ་བས་སྐུ་གསུམ་ཐོབ་འདོད་ཀྱི་འབྲས་བུ་མེད་དོ། །ཞེས་གསུངས་སོ། །

ཡ༽ བརྡ་ཉེར་བཞི་པ་ཨ་དཀར་ཐུགས་འཕོའི་བརྡ་བསྟན། ཡ༽ དོན་ཉེར་བཞི་པ་རང་བྱུང་ཡེ་ཤེས་སྐུར་ཐོབ་ས་ལམ་ལྟོས་པ་ཟད། རྒྱུ་འབྲས་བོན་ལ་མི་ལྟོས་མཁའ་ཁྱབ་དང་བའི་ངང་། རྐྱེན་གྱིས་བར་མ་ཆོད་ཅིང་གཉེན་པོས་གཞོམ་དུ་མེད། རིག་པ་རང་སར་གྲོལ་བས་འབྲས་བུ་སྐྱེ་འཇིག་བྲལ། ཞེས་གསུངས་སོ། །

22. Khandro Mahasukasitima showed the twenty-second symbol to Khandro Chöza Bönchigma, the sign of clasping her elbows, the essence of clarity.

As for the twenty-second meaning:

The Nature of Mind has neither past nor future, therefore it is connected to all the Buddhas of the three times. Immeasurable Compassion is encompassed within the Natural State, therefore it is connected with all the sentient beings of the three realms. If you know the Natural State is the source from which all things arise, abide and dissolve, it becomes conjoined with the path and result. If phenomena and emptiness are liberated into intrinsic awareness, the result will be obtained effortlessly.

Thus she spoke.

23. Chöza showed the twenty-third symbol, the sign of collecting the essential instructions of the Masters.

As for the twenty-third meaning:

The Natural State is not generated by causes or secondary causes, thus, firstly, it is primordially free of any basis for birth. It is the great indeterminate, therefore, secondly, there is no special place wherein it abides. Bönku is unchanging, thus, thirdly, there is no path for it to follow. Since all phenomena and whatever exists appear in the dimension of intrinsic awareness, there is no desire to attain the result of the three bodies.

Thus she spoke.

24. The twenty-fourth symbol is the sign of transferring the White A into the Natural State.[11]

As for the twenty-fourth meaning:

When the body of self-originated primordial wisdom is achieved, reliance upon the gradual path is utterly exhausted. Since this Nature depends on neither the Bön of Cause nor the Bön of Fruit, it is all-pervasive, like the vast expanse of the clear sky. Since it is undisturbed by secondary causes, it cannot be eliminated by antidotes. Since intrinsic awareness self-liberates, the result is free from creation and destruction.

Thus she spoke.

[11] I.e. Tib. 'pho ba.

ར༽ བརྡ་ཉེར་ལྔ་པ་སྤྱི་གཙུག་བླ་མའི་རྣལ་འབྱོར་བསྟན། ར༽ དོན་ཉེར་ལྔ་པ་རིག་པ་རང་བྱུང་ཡེ་ཤེས་འདི། རྒྱུ་རྐྱེན་སྐྱེ་འཇིག་ཡོད་མ་མྱོང་། ས་ལམ་འབྲས་བུ་བགྲང་བ་མེད། སྣང་རྟོག་བཅུ་བདུན་ཡུལ་ལས་གྲོལ། ཞེས་གསུངས་སོ།།

ལ༽ བརྡ་ཉེར་དྲུག་པ་རང་གསལ་འཕོར་ལོ་དྲུག་འགྱུར་གྱི་བརྡ་བསྟན། ལ༽ དོན་ཉེར་དྲུག་པ་དབྱིངས་ལས་ཡེ་ཤེས་ཐོག་བབས་ཤར་བས་ཐབ་བྱེད་རང་སར་གྲོལ། རྒྱུ་འབྲས་རིག་པ་ཐོག་བབས་ཤར་བས་ཐེག་པ་རང་སར་གྲོལ། སྐྱོན་སྣང་རིག་པ་ཐོག་བབས་ཤར་བས་འཛིན་བྱེད་རང་སར་གྲོལ། སྣང་སྟོང་རིག་པ་ཐོག་བབས་ཤར་བས་བྱེད་མཁན་རང་སར་གྲོལ། །ཞེས་གསུངས་སོ།།

25. The twenty-fifth symbol is the sign of venerating the lama on the crown of the head.

As for the twenty-fifth meaning:

This self-originated primordial wisdom-awareness has never been subject to cause, secondary cause, creation or destruction. Therefore, there is no enumeration of Bhumis, Paths or results. Thus it is liberated from being an object of the seventeen visions and of discursive thoughts.[12]

Thus she spoke.

26. The twenty-sixth symbol is the sign of turning the six self-clear wheels.

As for the twenty-sixth meaning:

Since Primordial Wisdom arises from the dimension of the Natural State suddenly like a thunderbolt, all causes of achievement self-liberate into their own nature. Moreover, since the Bön of Cause and the Bön of Fruit arise in intrinsic awareness suddenly like a thunderbolt, all vehicles self-liberate into their own nature. Since all impure visions arise in intrinsic awareness suddenly like a thunderbolt, the grasper self-liberates into its own nature. Since all phenomena and emptiness arise in intrinsic awareness suddenly like a thunderbolt, the creator self-liberates into its own nature.

Thus she spoke.

---

[12] I.e. the mistaken views of Dzogchen discussed in mDzad pa po Dag po Dran pa Nam mkha', *sNyan rgyud Rin po che nam mkha' 'phrul mdzod drang nges gnyis kyi gzhung cha lag dang bcas pa bzhugs,* Chapter: *rDzogs pa chen po snyan rgyud rin po che nam mkha' 'phrul gyi mdzod chen gyi 'grel ba bzhugs so* (Kathmandu: Library of Triten Norbutse Monastery, Deb phreng gsum pa 2004, First Edition), p. 260, lines 8-14; and *sPyi rgyud chen mo nam mkha' dkar po ye khri mtha' sel gyi gsung pod bzhugs,* Chapter: *Ye khri mtha' sel rgyud las dgos 'dod gsal byed bshad bzhi'i mchong*, (Kathmandu : Library of Triten Norbutse Monastery, Deb phreng 20, 2005) p. 314. For explanation in English see Yongdzin Lopön Tenzin Namdak Rinpoche. *Namkha Truldzö: the Commentary on the Precious Oral transmission of the Great Perfection which is called the Treasury of Space, Shenten Dargye Ling, 2 - 21 August 2005*, Trnscr. & ed. Carol Ermakova and Dmitry Ermakov (Blou, Shenten Dargye Ling, 2006), Week I, pp. 7-14; ibid. pp. 151-164; Gyaltsen, Shardza Tashi. Commentary by Lopon Tenzin Namdak, *Heart Drops of Dharmakaya: Dzogchen Practice of the Bön Tradition* (Ithaca: Snow Lion Publications, 1993), pp. 73, Footnote 33.

ཤ༽ བརྡ་ཉེར་བདུན་པ་གསལ་བྱེད་མེ་ལོང་ངོ་སྤྲོད་ཀྱི་བརྡ་བསྟན། ཤ༽ དོན་ཉེར་བདུན་པ་སེམས་ཀྱི་བོན་ཉིད་སྐྱེ་མེད་ལ། སྤྲོས་དང་མ་སྤྲོས་ཚིག་གི་ལམ། མཚན་མ་རྣམ་བཞིའི་ཡུལ་ལས་འདས། ཡོད་མཐོང་སྣང་གྲགས་རྫོགས་ཆེན་ལམ། ཞེས་གསུངས་སོ།།

ས༽ བརྡ་ཉེར་བརྒྱད་པ་ཕུང་པོ་ཚོགས་འབྱུལ་བརྡ་བསྟན། ས༽ དོན་ཉེར་བརྒྱད་པ་བདག་གྲོལ་སྟོང་པ་དོན་གྱི་བཅུད། ཕྱོགས་ལྷ་མགོ་མཉམ་གོལ་ས་ཡིན། རེ་དོགས་ཡོངས་བྲལ་རྩོལ་ལས་འདས། བོན་ཉིད་སྟོད་ཡངས་བདེ་བ་ཆེ། ཞེས་གསུངས་སོ།།

ཧ༽ བརྡ་ཉེར་དགུ་པ་སེང་གེ་རྣམ་གྲོལ་ཕྱུག་རྒྱུའི་བརྡ་བསྟན། ཧ༽ དོན་ཉེར་དགུ་པ་ཡེ་ཤེས་རྣམ་པར་དག་པས་འཁོར་བ་ཡི་མིང་ཡང་མེད། ཕུང་ལྷུ་མ་སྤྱངས་ཡེ་ནས་གདོད་སངས་རྒྱས། རིག་ཤེས་གསལ་བའི་རྒྱན་རྣམས་རྫོགས། ཀུན་བཟང་མཉམ་ཉིད་ཕྱོགས་མ་ལྷུང་། ཞེས་གསུངས་སོ།།

27. The twenty-seventh symbol is the sign of introducing the Natural State with a clear mirror.

As for the twenty-seventh meaning:

The Nature of Mind is unborn. Words can neither embellish nor simplify this essence of the Nature of Mind. It is free from the four characteristics of materiality: existing, seeing, appearing and being agreed reality. Such is the path of Dzogchen.

Thus she spoke.

28. The twenty-eighth symbol is the sign of offering the Tsok[13] of the body.

As for the twenty-eighth meaning:

The liberation of the self is the essence of emptiness. Holding biased views and drawing parallels is an error. The Natural State is totally free from expectations, doubts, and effort. It is the vast vessel; it is great bliss.

Thus she spoke.

29. The twenty-ninth symbol is the sign showing the seal of the essence of liberation, the Lion Posture.

As for the twenty-ninth meaning:

Primordial Wisdom is utterly pure therefore not even the name of Samsara exists. Without abandoning the five aggregates, primordial Buddhahood is realized. Everything is perfected as the adornment of clear wisdom-awareness. Kuntu Zangpo encompasses everything equally without falling into partiality.

Thus she spoke.

[13] Tib. tshogs. Here it refers to practice of Tib. gcod.

ཨ༔ བརྡ་ཤུམ་ཅུ་པ་དབང་རྗེ་ཁས་ཕུབ་ཀྱི་བརྡ་བསྟན། ཨ༔ དོན་ཤུམ་བཅུ་པ་འདི་ལ་མི་གནས་སྐལ་མེད་རྣམས། ཞོ་འདོད་རྣ་འཛོ་ཁྲི་ལྟེ་གནམ་ལ་སློག འབྱུང་བའི་བཀྲག་ཉམས་རག་ཤ་སྲིན་པོའི་གནས། བདུད་རྗི་དུག་དང་སྦྲུར་བས་སྐྱེ་འགྲོ་སྲོག་བཟུང་འཆད། ལྷ་བསྒོམ་སྤྱོད་འབྲས་འཚོལ་བས་འོར་མོ་ཁྲུང་དུ་འགྲོ། དམ་ཚིག་བཀའ་ཁྲིམས་ཉམས་པས་སྙིང་ཁྲག་ཁ་རུ་ལྷུག ཅེས་གསུངས་སོ། །ཤྲཱ་མཱ་ཡཱ་པ་ཏ། རྫོགས་སོ།། །།

30. The thirtieth symbol is the sign of the powerful lord's strong shield.

As for the thirtieth meaning:

All those unfortunate ones who do not realize this State are like a person who wants yoghurt but goes to milk a horn, or like a dog which wants to lick something but laps his tongue in space. This is the place of the Raksha flesh-eating demons where the lustre of the elements is dulled.

If you mix *düdtsi* with poison, you severe the life-force of beings. Similarly, if you err in the view, meditation, conduct and result, you fall from remaining in the Natural State into the pit of dark ignorance. If you break the Samaya and the commitment of this doctrine, it is as though your heart blood gushes from your mouth.

Thus she spoke.

Samaya pa ta!

Completed!

མཁས་པར་སྦྱངས་པའི་དྲན་པ་ནམ་མཁའ་བདག མོ་བརྒྱུད་དབུགས་འབྱིན་ཟངས་ཎོག་མཐིང་རིས་ཅན། མཁའ་འགྲོ་གྲུབ་ཐོབ་རིམ་པས་བརྒྱུད་པའི་བརྡ། ལས་ཅན་ཐར་པར་བགྲོད་ཕྱིར་ཕྱི་རབས་བུ་ལ་གཏད། རྒྱལ་བློན་གླེན་པས་བོན་བསྒྱུར་ཆོས་སུ་སྤྱོད། བསྟན་པའི་སྒྲོན་མེ་གཡུང་དྲུང་ས་འོག་སྦས། ཐུགས་ཀྱི་བརྒྱུད་པ་གསེར་དང་འདྲ་བ་འདི། གཏེར་དུ་མ་བསྐུབས་རང་གི་བརྒྱུད་ལ་དྲིལ། ལས་འཕྲོ་ཅན་རྣམས་ཐུགས་ནས་ཐུགས་སུ་ལྟོམས། བསྟན་པའི་སྙིང་ཡིན་ཀུན་གྱི་ཐུན་མོང་མིན། དམ་ཉམས་རྣམས་ལ་མ་གཟེམ་རང་གི་ཚེ་ལ་གནོད། ཅེས་གསུངས་སོ། །རྒྱ་རྒྱ་རྒྱ། རྒྱ་རྒྱ་རྒྱ། རྒྱ་རྒྱ་རྒྱ། རྒྱ་རིམ་པ་དགུ་ཡིས་བཏབ་བོ།

I am the learned scholar Drenpa Namkha. This living female lineage was inscribed with lapis lazuli on copper sheeting and is the symbol of the successive transmission through the lineage of Khandro and Drubthob. It is transmitted to disciples of future generations that fortunate ones may tread the path of liberation. Due to the foolishness of the king and ministers, Bön was transformed into Indian Buddha-Dharma practice. The lamp of the doctrine of Yungdrung Bön was hidden under the earth. However, this heart transmission, which is like gold, was not hidden as a terma but was always kept in my mind. Transmitted from the mind of one great fortunate successor to another, it has been kept alive. This is the heart essence of the doctrine which is not commonly shared. Do not give this to Samaya-breakers; doing so will harm your life.[14]

Thus he spoke.

Gya gya gya! Gya gya gya! Gya gya gya!

Sealed by nine seals!

---

[14] As is so often the case with esoteric teachings, the colophon to this text contains a word of caution to teachers to the effect that these pith instructions should not be taught indiscriminately. This then begs the question: should this book be available to the general public? When we put this to Yongdzin Rinpoche, he replied that it is indeed a difficult issue. Nowadays it is very hard to follow this advice as new technologies mean that texts are easily photocopied, scanned and distributed in many formats, so that even if a teacher requests his students to keep a particular text secret, it is often leaked and finds its way into the public domain. Recognizing this, Yongdzin Rinpoche entrusted us to make these precious teachings publicly available and has overseen the whole project, thus ensuring its integrity. He also reiterated that, according to the texts, it is sometimes permitted to teach Dzogchen openly. In this case, many people can hear about Dzogchen and this plants a karmic cause and a good connection for the future. If however, having heard a general discourse on Dzogchen, a student is interested and wishes to practise more seriously, the teacher must check very carefully whether the would-be student is indeed qualified to follow and practise Dzogchen.

།སོ་བརྒྱད་བརྡ་སུམ་བཅུ་པ། རྗེ་རི་ཁྲོད་པའི་ཐུགས་ཀྱི་ཐིགས་པ། སྤྲུལ་སྐུ་ལུང་སྟོན་ལྷ་གཞན་ལ་བརྒྱད། དེ་ཡིས་ལུང་སྒོམ་འཁོར་ལོ་རྒྱལ་པོ་ལ་བརྒྱད་པའོ།། ཨི་ཐིཿ

Tibetan text according to:

སྲིད་རྒྱུད་ཆེན་མོ་ནམ་མཁའ་དཀར་པོ་ཡེ་ཁྲི་མཐའ་སེལ་གྱི་གསུང་པོད་བཞུགས།།
ཁྲི་བརྟན་ནོར་བུ་རྩེའི་དཔེ་མཛོད་ཁང་གིས་དཔར་སྐྲུན་བྱས།
དེབ་ཕྲེང་ཉི་ཤུ་པ། 2005.

These thirty symbols and meanings of the female lineage, the heart essence of the lord hermit, were transmitted to Trulku Lungton Lhanyen who transmitted them to Lunggom Khorlo Gyalpo.

Translated by Nagru Geshe Gelek Jinpa, Carol Ermakova and Dmitry Ermakov, Shenten Dargye Ling, Blou, France, March 2011.

མཁའ་འགྲོ་ཅོ་ཟ་བོན་མོའི་གསོལ་འདེབས།

PRAYER TO KHANDRO CHÖZA BÖNMO

བསམ་ཡས་ཧས་པོ་རི་ཡི་སྒྲུབ་གནས་སུ།
SAM YE HI PO RI YI DRUB NE SU
In the hermitage of Samye Hipo Ri

།ཅི་ཡང་མ་ངེས་སྒྱུ་མ་ལྷ་མོའི་སྐུ།
CHI YANG MA NGE GYU MA LHA MÖ KU
Is the manifestation of the illusory body of the goddess

།སྦྱངས་ཤུགས་སྟོབས་ཀྱིས་ལྷག་མེད་མངོན་སངས་རྒྱས།
JYANG SHUK TOB KYI LHAK ME NGON SANG GYE
Who through the power of practice, achieved Buddhahood without leaving any (physical) remains.

།རྒྱལ་བའི་ཡུམ་གྱུར་ཅོ་ཟ་བོན་མོ་ལ།
GYAL WAI YUM GYUR CHÖ ZA BÖN MO LA
To you, Chöza Bönmo, great mother of the Buddhas, to you,

།དགའ་བདེའི་ངང་དུ་བདག་ཉིད་གསོལ་བ་འདེབས།
GA DEI NGANG DU DAG NYI SOL WA DEB
I pray with blissful joy.

།དུས་གསུམ་སངས་རྒྱས་བསྐྱེད་པ་རིན་པོ་ཆེ།
DÜ SUM SANG GYE KYED PA RIN PO CHE
You who are the precious manifestation of the Buddhas of the three times,

།མཆོག་ཐུན་དངོས་གྲུབ་རྫོགས་པར་བྱིན་གྱིས་རློབས།།
CHOK THÜN NGÖ DRUB DZOG PAR JYIN GYI LOB
Please bless me that I may fully achieve the common *siddhi* and the realization of supreme Buddhahood!

Taken from Dzogchen Yangtse Longchen.

Translated by Nagru Geshe Gelek Jinpa, Carol Ermakova and Dmitry Ermakov, Dolianova, Sardegna, 20 December, 2010.

Khandro Chöza Bönchigma

THE LAMP OF THE FORTUNATE MIND

A hagiography of Khandro Chöza Bönmo

Without wavering from the Natural State in any of the three times, you manifested clearly to liberate sentient beings and protect the doctrines.
Enjoying the great secret practice of uniting method and wisdom, you brought all the Drubthob-*yogis into the four joys.*

Ripening the essence of contemplation and bliss within your mind, you liberated desire for the eight worldly concerns into the great dimension of the Natural State.
Being fully familiar with the four stages of thögal *visions and the base,*
You, great Chöza Bönchigma, the sole mother of the doctrine,
Realized Rainbow Body without leaving any remains.

Having fully realized the yidam *of the Natural State, you utterly exhausted any mental judgements about emptiness.*
By means of the pure primordial wisdom wind, innate joy and heat arose in your mind,
The sixteen groups of thigles *settled in your three channels and five chakras, and,*
By means of the thigles *dropping and rising miraculously, you realized the union of great bliss and primordial wisdom.*

Although words fail to fully describe
Your deeds of the four activities,
Please grant me, the one who devotedly wishes to enter the path,
Permission to tell your story.

After our Lord Buddha Tönpa Shenrab achieved the excellent three bodies, he took rebirth in the central southern island, the human realm, to teach the doctrines and benefit all sentient beings, firmly establishing the three doctrines of Do, Ngag and Dzogchen.[1] Countless disciples appeared among the gods, nagas and humans and, following Buddha Tönpa Shenrab, they practised the great teachings of Bön Do, Ngag or Dzogchen according to their capacity. Over the ages, many accomplished male and female practitioners have achieved Buddhahood and attained the great realization of *siddhi* through practising these teachings. During the lifetime of Buddha Tönpa Shenrab himself, many great *yoginis* – such as Shenza Neuchen, Shenza Neuchung, and Lumo Mamade[2] – were entrusted with keeping his doctrines. These numerous women who held the lineages of Sutra, Tantra and Dzogchen performed many marvellous deeds for the benefit of sentient beings and to ensure the continuation of the teachings.

Later, the threefold collection of Bön Do, Ngag and Dzogchen spread into the highest countries on this earth, the culturally rich lands of Zhang Zhung and Tibet. During the initial phase of propagation, there were nine *Drubthobma*[3] – women *mahasiddhas* – who achieved the great *siddhi* of realization here. Others followed in their footsteps, and many *yoginis*[4] subsequently attained the full result of Do, Ngag and Dzogchen. Our historical records bear witness to this.

The second phase or spread of Buddha Tönpa Shenrab's doctrines into Zhang Zhung and Tibet took place in the eighth century. This was a time when a great number of accomplished female Dzogchen practitioners held the lineages of the essential teachings of Do, Ngag and Dzogchen. In particular, there were the four Bönmo tamers of the borderlands and the six *Drubthobma* who lived in this area in those days. These women achieved the three Buddha bodies[5] in that very lifetime, showing wonderful signs of realization and displaying inconceivable magical powers. The four Bönmo protectresses of the borderlands were:[6]

---

[1] Tib. mdo sngags sems gsum - is often translated as Sutra, Tantra and Dzogchen. However, in the Bön tradition *mdo* cannot be described as Sutra alone since many *mdo* texts contain the teachings of Sutra, Tantra and Dzogchen.

[2] Tib. gShen za Ne'u chen, gShen za Ne'u chung, Klu mo Ma ma de.

[3] Tib. grub thob rdzu 'phrul ma dgu.

[4] Tib. rnal 'byor ma.

[5] Tib. sku gsum.

[6] Tib. sa mtshams srung ba'i bon mo bzhi.

1. Bönmo Ganga Gongchung[7] from Upper Tsang[8] who stayed in the region between Mon[9] and Tibet;
2. Bönmo Jyorra Jyordzong from Chiymen[10] who stayed on the border between Dendrug[11] and Tibet;
3. Dangdragma of the Chaza clan[12] who stayed in the borderlands between Zhang Zhung and Tibet;
4. Monmo Shibshinggi Ngulmoche[13] who stayed in the region between the grassmen and woodmen[14] and Tibet.

These four women were known as the four Bönmo guardians of the borderlands; they stayed in outlying regions and subdued them.

As for the six great Bön ladies, the six Drubthobma:[15] the first was Tsomengyal of the Shen clan.[16] Her accomplishment was that, when she raised the offering above the crown of her head, the wisdom divinities would manifest visibly to receive it. The second was Ngachunggyal of the Zhu clan.[17] As for her accomplishment, whenever she wanted to go somewhere, she would simply think of the place, close her eyes, and meditate, and she would arrive there. The third great lady, Ngagza Tipang,[18] possessed the *siddhi* of leaping on her drum and flying through space without ever falling down. Rachagza Yanggyalma's[19] achievement was that she could mount the horse of her *shang*[20] and soar to the peak of a snow mountain to practise sun-gazing. Böntsolma of the Nanam

[7] Tib. Bon mo Gang nga Gong chung.
[8] Tib. gTsang stod.
[9] Tib. Mon.
[10] Tib. sKyid sman.
[11] Tib. Dhan drug - it is not entirely clear where this location is; it may refer to Himalayan borderlands or India.
[12] Tib. Ca za'i gDang grags ma.
[13] Tib. Mon mo Shib shing gi dNgul mo che.
[14] Tib. rtsa mi shing mi. According to Yongdzin Rinpoche and Geshe Gelek, this probably refers to tiny humans who are said to live somewhere in the far North of the Tibetan Plateau, before reaching the flatlands beyond the northern mountains, controlled by proto-Mongol tribes in those times. They are said to be 'fairy folk' only a few inches high, who shoot arrows made of grass at humans trespassing into their terrain so that, should you go there, you will find your socks full of grass. The grass can be used for herbal medicine.
[15] Tib. bon mo grub thob ma drug.
[16] Tib. gShen za mTsho sman rgyal.
[17] Tib. Zhu za rNga chung rgyal.
[18] Tib. sNgags za Ti pang.
[19] Tib. Ra lcags za Yang rgyal ma.
[20] Tib. gshang - Bönpo flat bell.

clan[21] achieved the *siddhi* of wrapping Lake Mapang in the hem of her skirt without spilling a drop. And Chöza Bönmo[22] achieved the *siddhi* of tying a dried deer antler into nine knots.

There were many such accomplished Bönmo who possessed miraculous powers and blessings. Their names and deeds are clearly recorded in *Dragpa Lingdrag*.[23]

Here, I would like to write about the life of one of these great ladies, Chöza Bönmo. Although many tales are told about this amazing woman who realized the Rainbow Body of the Great Transfer,[24] I am basing this biography on the teaching texts. We know for a fact that Chöza Bönmo was a Tibetan woman who lived in the eighth century and was renowned as a practitioner of Dzogchen. It was to her that the great Bön Dzogchen Master Drenpa Namkha[25] entrusted the female Dzogchen lineage. Chöza Bönmo was also the secret consort and main disciple of both Lachen Drenpa Namkha and Nyachen Lishu Tagring,[26] from whom she received the profound instructions on the union of Tantra and Dzogchen.[27]

This unusual woman is mentioned quite often in our historical texts. For instance, it is recorded that Lachen Drenpa Namkha taught the Bönpo Dzogchen teachings of *Yetri Thasel*[28] and *Ngedon Namkha Truldzö*[29] to the Tibetan King Trisong Deutsen,[30] the great translator Vairochana,[31] and Chöza Bönmo. We also know that Chöza Bönmo was a very close spiritual friend of King Trisong Deutsen, while the historical annals of Zhang Zhung and Tibet name her as having achieved the Rainbow Body of the Great Transfer in the support of a woman's body.

Her birth

Chöza Bönmo is the emanation of the great mother Zangza Ringtsün.[32] To uphold the doctrines for the benefit of all sentient

[21] Tib. sNa nam za Bon tshol ma.
[22] Tib. Co za Bon mo.
[23] *bsGrags pa gling grags*, *Exalted Proclamation in the World*, pp. 67-68, *brTen 'gyur*, vol. 72, published by Sog sde sPrul sku bsTan pa'i Nyi ma.
[24] Tib. 'ja' lu 'pho ba chen po.
[25] Tib. Bla chen Dran pa Nam mkha'.
[26] Tib. sNya chen Li shu sTag ring.
[27] Tib. *sNgags rdzogs zung 'brel.*
[28] Tib. *sPyi rgyud chen mo ye khri mtha' sel.*
[29] Tib. Nges don nam mkha' 'phrul mdzod.
[30] Tib. Khri srong lDe'u btsan.
[31] Tib. Lo chen Bai ro tsa na.
[32] Tib. bZang za Ring btsun.

beings, she took birth in the eighth century in a place called Dagpo Sazho.[33] Her father was called Gyimbu Lantsha of the Chö clan[34] and her mother was called Damocham.[35] When Chöza was still in her mother's womb, the sound of Ha and Phat could be heard radiating from her. While Damocham was with child, she dreamt many auspicious dreams and wonderful rainbow lights would sometimes fill the house. Many similar auspicious signs appeared. Chöza's birth was greeted by a host of Dakinis, including the pig-faced Khandro of Nödjin[36] as well as many other flesh-eating Dakinis who circumambulated the newborn baby. Through the power of positive karma and virtuous past lives, Chöza was naturally disinclined towards desire, and endowed with wisdom. As she grew up, she easily mastered reading, writing and reciting without the need for study. She was stunningly beautiful, and her mind was naturally calm and quiet. In particular, Chöza had the four special signs which made her unlike other human girls: her body was decorated with marks of lotuses and other flowers; she naturally gave off the scent of aloe vera and sandalwood; the sound of her name would ring out early in the morning, but there was no-one to be seen; when it was time for the morning and evening meal, a small *chogtritra*[37] bird would chirp to call her to eat. In her dreams, she would give alms and many different objects of enjoyment; the Shenpo knowledge holders from Zhang Zhung and India would confer empowerments and teachings on her; she would offer *tsok*,[38] ride a Garuda,[39] and travel to the realm of the Thirty-Three Gods to make offerings there.

Meeting her Root Master

When Chöza was a bit older, her parents decided the time had come for her to marry. So they bought many precious turquoise ornaments, bedecked her in sumptuous golden jewellery, and sent her to meet her future husband at a betrothal party attended by many young people. Chöza, however, did not want to go, preferring

[33] Tib. Dag po Tsa shod.

[34] Tib. Co Gyim bu Lan tsha.

[35] Tib. bDa' mo lcam. She was also called rGya mo skyid lcam, Happy Lady of the Seal, as is clearly stated in the *Drang don mun sel sgron ma, The Lamp which Clarifies the Provisional Meaning*, Chapter *gTam rgyud brda yi gzer bu, The Symbolic Nail of Oral History*, p. 92, published by Khri brtan Nor bu rtse'i dpe mdzod khang, Kathmandu: 2004.

[36] Tib. gNod sbyin gyi mkha' 'gro.

[37] Tib. lcog kri kras.

[38] Tib. tshogs mchod. Skt. ganapuja.

[39] Tib. khyung.

to stay alone. This was a sign that she was disgusted by *samsara* and her mind was free from all worldly concerns.

Meanwhile, the great royal Bön lama[40] Drenpa Namkha, an emanation of Tseme Wöden,[41] had recognized Chöza Bönmo as an emanation of the great mother Zangza Ringtsün, so, disguising himself as a beggar, he went to the house of the Cho family asking for alms.

"Please! Spare me some food!" he called out.

When Chöza heard him, she picked up a wooden plate full of *tsampa* and went to the door. As soon as she saw Lachen Drenpa Namkha's face, she was overcome with joy. Her whole body trembled uncontrollably and as she offered the plate of *tsampa* to him with a shaking hand, it slipped from her fingers and broke in two. The barley flour spilt all over the ground. Lachen Drenpa Namkha said to her:

Lachen Drenpa Namkha

"You have broken the plate! Now you must share half of all your property and food with me. If not, you must give me one bright, priceless treasure."

Chöza didn't tell her parents she had broken the plate. Stealthily creeping back into the house, she stole a whole cheese and a ribcage, then tiptoed back to the doorway.

"So? What have you got for me?" asked the lama.

She offered him the stolen victuals and asked him for a blessing. From that moment on, she felt great respect and

[40] Tib. Bla chen.

[41] Tib. Tshad med 'Od ldan.

unequivocal devotion towards him.

Chöza's parents still wanted her to marry. They had a long talk with her, trying to persuade her she must wed the wealthy suitor. But Chöza replied:

"All phenomena of *samsara* are devoid of essence!"

And so saying, she refused to go and be married. Feigning madness, she tried to avoid the wedding, but to no avail. Finally, when the time for her to be sent to her groom-to-be was almost upon her, she ran away into the red rocky crags of Samye.[42] Her relatives tried in vain to seize her, but they could not bring her back. And so it was that she stayed in a solitary place practising the preliminary practices which turn one's mind from *samsara*, and engaging in the three studies of listening, reflecting upon the meaning, and meditating.

How she practised great, unsurpassable Dzogchen

Chöza met the great Bönpo Dzogchen master Lishu Tagring from whom she received *Dzogchen Dragpa Korsum*[43] in full, as well as teachings on both the provisional and ultimate meaning of *Dzogpa Chenpo Yangtse Longchen*.[44] Lishu Tagring then gave her instructions and introduced her to the Natural State. This is what he said:

> "*Listen, Khandro, the emanation of primordial wisdom!*"

And he gave her the empowerment Gyaltheb Chyilug.[45]

> "*Assume the* mudra *of the natural body posture with the gaze like that of a lion, and let your mind focus in space. This non-conceptual state is beyond elaboration, thought and words. Leave it just as it is, fresh, relaxed and uncorrected. This is the essence of Kuntu Zangpo. This is the direct introduction. Have confidence in it!*"

Such were his words.[46]

[42] Tib. bSam yas.
[43] Tib. *rDzogs chen bsgrags pa skor gsum*.
[44] Tib. *rDzogs pa chen po yongs rtse klong chen*.
[45] Tib. rGyal thebs spyi lugs - a special introduction-initiation which is given to a person so that s/he can become the successor of the lineage. It belongs to the last of the Four Initiations, Tib. dbang bzhi.
[46] From *rDzogs pa chen po yongs rtse klong chen*, *The Essential Point of*

Chöza Bönmo practised exactly as Lama Lishu had taught her and gained a direct realization of the Natural State. Then, from the top of Mount Hipori,[47] she sang the following song of experience:

E MA HO!
Marvellous!
How wondrous! There, where there is neither day nor night, the sun of constant clarity shines.
I, the Lady of yoginis, warm myself with its heat!
Introducing the doctrines to my mind – this is the great kindness of my master
Looking with my mind towards my mind – this is the great kindness to myself!

If you fail to sever the fetters of samsara, your determination to reach the Pure Land will never be realized
If you fail to liberate defiling thoughts, your determination to reach the Pure Land will never be realized
If you do not capture and jail the king, you will surely fail to subdue the soldiers.[48]
Firmly mount the beam of Lungdrug[49] *in the castle of the View of Great Perfection*
Crown it with the battlement of the eight pith instructions.[50]

Having readied the bow of the clear Nature of Mind,
Let fly the arrow of the four short instructions,[51]
And having directly pierced the wooden shield of the five poisons,
Liberate the beings of the six samsaric realms
And gain victory over the opponent, delusion.

---

the Great Expanse of the Great Perfection, *rGyal thebs spyi lugs kyi dbang*, p. 54, sMad cha (Vol. II), published by Triten Norbutse Library (Khri brten nor bu rtse'i dpe mdzod khang), printed by Si khron mi rigs dpe skrun khang, 2008.

[47] Tib. Has po ri.

[48] I.e. if you don't control your mind, you will not be able to control discursive thoughts.

[49] Tib. *Lung drug* - Dzogchen teachings from *bsGrags pa skor gsum*.

[50] Tib. *Man ngag brgyad* - Dzogchen teachings from *bsGrags pa skor gsum*.

[51] Tib. *Yig chung bzhi* - Dzogchen teachings from *bsGrags pa skor gsum*.

If the enemies – desire and anger – are not eliminated,
You will be powerless to protect the glorious child of the mind.
If you do not stop the great river of the three poisons,
The fire of primordial wisdom will lack the power to blaze.
If you do not shun samsaric companions,
The horse of great happiness will lack the power to gallop.
If you do not separate yourself from attachment to children, relatives and friends,
The great vulture of your own mind will lack the power to soar in the sky.
If you do not fell the trunk of discursive thoughts,
The leaves of samsara will proliferate.
If you do not separate yourself from the enemies, the five poisons,
They will lead you into the pit of darkness.
If you do not destroy even the subtlest attachment to your body,
You will remain integrated with this body of affliction.
If you do not set alight the lamp of primordial wisdom,
It will be smothered by the descending darkness of ignorance.

Since I have the castle of the Dzogchen View,
I do not fear the army of afflictive emotions!
Since I have immutable, unfailing armour,
I do not fear the weapons of the five poisons!
Since I have Yeshe Sempas[52] *as my companions,*
I do not fear parting with loved ones!
Since all pleasures are encompassed within my mind,
I do not fear relinquishing my possessions!
Separating from everything is excellent happiness!
Staying alone is excellent happiness!
Freedom from companions is excellent happiness!
My great kind Masters introduced Bön to my mind!

[52] Tib. lha ye shes sems dpa' - 'wisdom being divinity,' one of the Tib. sems dpa' sum of Bönpo Tantra. The two others are: Tib. bdag dam tshig sems dpa' - 'one's own being of spiritual commitment;' and Tib. gnyis med las kyi sems dpa' - 'non-dual action being.'

My great kind Masters liberated me from the mire of samsara!
My great kind Masters utterly dried the lake of afflictive emotions!
My great kind Masters showed me how to achieve Buddhahood in my mind!
I am Chöza Bönmo, the sole mother of the doctrine, she who has realized the Nature of her own mind!
I watch the play of my own mind
I seek my life-companion within my mind
I am Chöza Bönmo, she who enjoys the pleasures of her own mind!
My view is like space
My conduct is like the earth
My meditation is like a butter lamp
My instructions are like nectar;
All you beings suffering in samsara -
If you hanker after a lord, take the yidam as your lord.
If you hanker after a life-companion, take your own mind as your partner.
If you hanker after servants, take the Protectors as your servants.
If you hanker after enjoyment, take the melodies of Bön as your enjoyment.
If you want to watch something, watch your mind.
If you want to make offerings, offer to the five Buddha families.
If you want to meditate, meditate on non-conceptual wisdom.
If you want to stay somewhere, stay in a place of solitude!

This is the song Chöza Bönmo sang on top of Mount Hipori.

Then, arriving at the final stage of meditation, she achieved Buddhahood.

Thus it is said.[53]

---

[53] From *The Three Cycles of Dzogchen Proclamation (rDzogs chen bsgrags pa skor gsum)* in the *Tengyur (brTen 'gyur) Collection*, p. 256, Vol. 113, published by Sog sde sPrul sku bsTan pa'i Nyi ma.

As mentioned above, Chöza Bönmo also received *Yetri Thasel* and the Dzogchen cycle of instructions called *Namkha Truldzö* from Lachen Drenpa Namkha as well as the complete four initiations, and the direct introduction – Rigpa Tsalwang.[54] She went on to practise these until her mind was fully ripened and she attained complete liberation. Although the main focus of her study was listening to and reflecting upon *Dragpa Korsum*, it was when she received the Dzogchen teachings of *Namkha Truldzö* that the experience of the Base of the primordial awareness of instant self-liberation arose in her. In addition, Lachen Drenpa Namkha also gave Chöza Bönmo the instructions on the direct introduction called the three pith instructions of Gyunne,[55] constant abiding.

This is how he introduced her: [56]

> *Chöza! Look in space!*
> *Clouds appear by themselves and liberate by themselves.*
> *Yesterday's cloud is not a cloud today;*
> *The cloud of the morning is no longer a cloud now.*
> *Clouds are temporary and liberate by themselves.*
> *Therefore that which obstructs is devoid of essence.*
> *The vast sky does not reject clouds;*
> *It remains constant, naturally free from obscurations.*
> *Look at all the myriad external appearances – white, red or whatever they may be.*[57]
> *Whatever appears as an enemy is not an enemy;*
> *Whatever appears as a relative is not a relative;*
> *Enemies or relatives alike are but temporary, deluded apparitions.*
> *When temporary appearances self-liberate, such visions are seen to be without essence,*
> *Thus visions are great liberation.*
> *Without renouncing deluded visions, the Natural State remains primordially free.*
> *Look at the internal grasper and the thoughts it seizes!*

[54] Tib. rig pa rtsal dbang.
[55] Tib. rgyun gnas.
[56] Taken from *The Key of the Essential Pith Instructions (Man ngag gnad kyi lde mig)*, p. 226, from *The Miraculous Treasury of the Sky (Nam mkha' 'phrul gyi mdzod chen)*, composed by Drenpa Namkha (Dran pa Nam mkha'), published by Triten Norbutse Library (Khri brten nor bu rtse'i dpe mdzod khang).
[57] I.e. anything.

Both grasper and thoughts are but temporary mind.
When this temporary grasper self-liberates, it is recognized as being devoid of actual reality.
Thus the grasper is great liberation.
Without renouncing either the grasper or discursive thoughts, the Natural State remains primordially free.
As for the three absences:
The Natural State is beyond the body – it has neither colour nor substance;
The Natural State is beyond speech – it has never been the object of words;
The Natural State is beyond thought – it has never been either the apprehended or the indicative object.

Thus he instructed her.

All the impure thoughts and mental stains of Chöza's mind were dissolved into great non-grasping self-liberation and the primordial wisdom of self-awareness arose clearly and nakedly.

Nyachen Lishu Tagring

Then Chöza dedicated herself to practice on Mount Hipori and obtained both common and supreme *siddhi*. She attained the miraculous power of swift walking: with just three steps, she could circumambulate the entire mountain. She was also able to tie nine knots in the dried antler of a deer. Through the power of her contemplation, she was able to invite the Masters and they would come. Completely renouncing worldly food, she sustained herself on the elixir of contemplation and practised unsurpassable Dzogchen. This is how she lived.

During this period, the Base of everything manifested directly in Chöza's mind and merged inseparably with her awakened awareness of primordial wisdom. But in order to cultivate the final stage on the path of Trekchö[58] and rip open the visions of the clear light of spontaneous perfection, she stayed in the dark practising unsurpassable Dzogpa Chenpo.

This is clear from the following instructions she received from Lama Lishu Tagring:[59]

> *'These instructions on unifying the Clear Light with the Base are the powerful method by which you can achieve Buddhahood.*
> *In the dark, visions of light appear from the dimension of the Natural State; the radiance of great primordial wisdom arises.*
> *If you meditate and familiarize yourself with this state, there is no need to strive towards Buddhahood.'*

Chöza practised in precisely this way and went on to achieve the final stage on the path of Trekchö.

Lishu Tagring then gave her the instructions on the spontaneous perfection of Clear Light, the practice of Thögal.[60] She practised this and achieved the fourth level of Thögal, the exhaustion of visions. Then Chöza attained the Rainbow Body of the great transfer.

This is what he taught her: [61]

> *'O emanation of the Khandro of primordial wisdom, purify the visions of delusion by means of the five pure lands.*
> *Liberate material aggregates by means of the five Buddha families.*

[58] Tib. khregs chod.

[59] From *rGyal thebs dbang khrid gnad kyi lag len*, from *rDzogs chen yongs rtse klong chen*, p. 146, published by Triten Norbutse Library, printed by Si khron mi rigs dpe skrun khang, 2008.

[60] Tib. thod rgal.

[61] From *rDzogs pa chen po yongs rtse klong chen, dGongs rgyud drug gi klad don nyi shu rtsa bdun nyams kyi man ngag gnad kyi yig chung*, p. 28, sMad cha (Vol. II), published by Triten Norbutse Library, printed by Si khron mi rigs dpe skrun khang, 2008.

Condense the objects of dualistic mind into the Natural State by means of the five lights.
Practise the absolute certainty that all this is none other than the five wisdoms.
As for the three deluded visions of sounds, lights and rays,
Have absolute confidence that the three bodies are within your own Nature of Mind.
In this life, practise and familiarize yourself with the Nature of your own Mind.
Chains of awareness, thigles, *divinities and mandalas appear as the inner signs of accomplishment,*
When the time comes for this apparent body of the five elements to disintegrate, leave behind this shell you have borrowed from the five elements.
The five Buddhas are the luminous essence of the five lights.
The self-luminous essence of the Nature of Mind is free from acceptance and rejection.
By the skilful means of drawing the chain of awareness of the five lights, lift the awareness-Hung in the pathway of the central channel.
Condense sounds, rays and lights in the swastika of Kuntu Zangpo's heart,
Thus the unimpeded wisdom awareness of truly awakened Buddhahood manifests.'

These were his instructions.

Then Chöza Bönmo practised exactly as she had been taught, and all the aggregates of her apparent physical body as well as all ordinary visions, both gross and subtle, were unequivocally liberated into the dimension of the essential nature of the Great Ancestor, the Base. Then Chöza manifested the excellent body of unsullied wisdom.

The great deeds Chöza performed for the doctrines and the benefit of all sentient beings

Although the fortunes of the Bön doctrines waxed and waned in Tibet over the centuries between the reigns of the first king of Tibet, Nyatri Tsenpo,[62] and the eighth-century king, Trisong Deutsen,[63]

[62] Tib. gNya' khri bTsan po.
[63] Tib. Khri srong lDe'u btsan.

by and large Bön was practised throughout the kingdom. As a young man, King Trisong Deutsen himself entered the path of Bön; historical records clearly state that he received and practised the cycles of the provisional and ultimate meaning of Dzogchen *Namkha Truldzö* from Drenpa Namkha:[64]

> *The two oral traditions, the teachings I hold in my heart, were given to five disciples of noble families in whom the excellent qualities had come together. It is said that three – Vairochana, the mighty King, and Chöza Bönmo – will attain supreme* siddhi *and manifest Buddhahood.*

In fact, this portrayal of King Trisong Deutsen differs quite considerably from those found elsewhere. I would suggest that these differing opinions can be traced back to differing religious outlooks. Tibetan followers of Indian Buddhism tended to see such figures as Tibetan ministers who practised Bön or the Tibetan King Lhase Langdarma[65] as the main hindrance for the spread of Indian Buddhism in Tibet, dubbing them 'evil ministers,' 'the evil king' and so on. In a similar way, when King Trisong Deutsen practised the doctrines of Bön, Bönpos referred to him as an emanation of Buddha, but when he went on to persecute Bön, he is described as being possessed by nasty Gyalgong[66] spirits.

Later in his rule, acquiescing to the wishes of sages such as Lopön Pema Jyungne[67] and Khenpo Boddhi Satto[68] invited from India and China, as well as to pressure from Dharma ministers of Tibet, King Trisong Deutsen set out to destroy the doctrines of Yungdrung Bön, the specifically Tibetan tradition which originated here in the Land of Snows and comprises Sutra, Tantra and Dzogchen. And so it was that Tibetans themselves perpetrated a cultural revolution in their own land. It was a time of devastation; a vast number of scriptures pertaining to Yungdrung Bön were burnt. Others were tossed into the rivers or scattered to the four

[64] From *Drang don mun sel sgron ma, The Lamp which clarifies the Provisional Meaning,* Chapter *gTam rgyud brda yi gzer bu The Symbolic Nail of Oral History*, p. 32, published by Triten Norbutse Library.

[65] Tib. Lha sras gLang Dar ma.

[66] Tib. rgyal 'gong - a class of malevolent spirits born of the union of Tib. rgyal po and Tib. sren mo sprirts, who provoke practitioners to break their spiritual commitments.

[67] Tib. sLob dpon Pad ma 'Byung gnas - i.e. Padmasambhava.

[68] Tib. mKhan po Bho ti sa two - i.e. Abbot Shantirakshita.

winds. Bönpo *gompas*[69] were laid waste while the three supports[70] of the Buddha's body, speech and mind were destroyed, and Bön lamas, ministers and powerful noble people as well as ordinary folk were put to death or banished. Their property was confiscated by the government and those who remained in Tibet were forcefully – and sometimes brutally – converted to the new religion, Indian Buddhism. As a result of these severe measures, Chöza Bönmo was the sole person practising pure, unadulterated Bön in central Tibet.

When King Trisong Deutsen launched the persecution of the Bönpos, the great Shen *yogis* and *yoginis*[71] gathered together in council and decided to hide a number of holy Bönpo scriptures. As for the rest, they decided to preserve some by replacing Bön names and terms with Indian Buddhist ones – converting the Bön scriptures into Indian Buddhist ones, as it were. Others were modified to make them similar to Indian Buddhist texts. Over time, this led to the development of the *terma*[72] system, oral traditions[73] and the New Bön School.[74]

Unlike the other Shen *yogis* and *yoginis*, Chöza Bönmo did not leave her homeland. It may be because she was King Trisong Deutsen's close spiritual friend, or because she possessed miraculous powers, or because she completely renounced worldly affairs and dedicated her life to living in solitude, but for whatever reason, she was the sole person who remained in Central Tibet practising Bön in these critical times. And this is really quite amazing!

Countless miseries and misfortunes befell Tibet during this difficult period, and, troubled, King Trisong Deutsen paid a visit to Chöza's hermitage at a place called Kharchen Dragkar.[75] the Great Castle of the White Crag.

> *The King enquired of the Lady Chöza, asking the reason for all the troubles.*
> *The Lady of Bön replied:*
> *"O King, this is your doing!*

[69] Tib. dgon pa - either a temple, practice retreat centre, hermitage or monastery.
[70] Tib. rten gsum - statues and *thangkas* for the body, texts for the speech and *chörtens* for the mind.
[71] Tib. Bon gshen rig 'dzin mkha' 'gro - highly realized male and female masters of Yungdrung Bön.
[72] Tib. gter ma - rediscovered spiritual texts hidden during times of persecution and turmoil.
[73] Tib. snyan rgyud.
[74] Tib. bon gsar ma.
[75] Tib. mKhar chen brag dkar.

You accepted what should not be accepted!
You completely destroyed blessed fortunate Bön! You banished the Bönpos and rejected Bön! That is the cause of these troubles. Moreover, three years hence, your royal kingdom will be no more."

Again he asked her, saying:
"What can we do to remedy this?"

She answered, saying:
"Invite all the yogis and Shenpo and allow them to practise Bön! As for the king and all his ministers, you should propitiate the Gurlha and Polha,[76] the original protective and ancestral gods. Perform Sel[77] exorcism rituals and offer the great Sangchö[78] so as to make great peace among all beings in the universe."

She spoke in no uncertain terms, telling him:
"Do this and it will help!"

Then the King realized the truth of her words. He called a council to discuss how to best invite the Shenpos and persuade them to return. One of the council members declared that the yogis *had all perished in the northern wastelands and no-one was left alive.*

But Chöza, the Lady of Bön, spoke up, saying:
"The Shenpo yogis *are all in the high pastures of the North where they are served by the wrathful red-eyed rock-spirits.[79] They sip the milk from the graceful deer and other comely wild animals. They are alive. If you listen to whatever these Shen* yogis *tell you and sign a royal decree granting them special standing, then I will invite them."*

[76] Tib. mgur lha, pho lha.
[77] Tib. sel.
[78] Tib. bsang mchod.
[79] Tib. brag srin mig dmar.

The King Trisong Deutsen gave his word that he would act in accordance with her advice, saying: "Very well then, go and bring them!"

And he handed her jars brimming with gold and silver as an offering for the yogis.

Riding a nine-legged mule[80] *and ceaselessly making offerings to the gods, Chöza galloped off. When she met the* yogis *of Shen, she told them of the troubles plaguing Tibet and that she had come to invite them back, asking them to please return.*

Chetsa Kharbu[81] *from Menyag said: "The sole purpose of Bön is to benefit sentient beings, so out of compassion, we will go."*

He said this, and all the Shen yogis *set off. When the Shenpo arrived at the palace, the King and yogis greeted each other with equal respect.*

Firstly, the yogis *of Shen spoke as one, saying: "A sekang-temple*[82] *must be built to subdue the Gyalgong spirits!"*
And so a sekhang *was erected in the place called Pekar Ling.*[83] *Furthermore, a black* chörten[84] *was built according to the Bön tradition. All the* yogis *performed the To*[85] *rituals for averting misfortunes, and together with all the ministers, the King propitiated the Gurlha and Polha protective and ancestral gods of the royal lineage. The divinities turned their face towards them, and the waters of the Yarlung River abated. Drenpa Namkha was released from his previous forced abjuration of his religion and conferred a long-life initiation upon the King, thus curing him from his sickness. All the various diseases and unrest ceased*

[80] Tib. Dre'u 'phar ma dgu rkang. I.e. she rode very fast thanks to her magical powers.
[81] Tib. Me nyag lCe tsha mKhar bu.
[82] Tib. gsas khang.
[83] Tib. Pe dkar gling.
[84] Tib. mchod rten nag po.
[85] Tib. gto.

> *throughout Tibet. The King rejoiced and bestowed glorious official titles upon the Bönpos, offering them three regions in the upper lands of Tibet: Zage Serteng; Tsangpo Zhungme and Chubar Drona.*[86] *He offered them three regions in the lower lands of Tibet: Wolmo Lungrung, Phenyul Dramchye and Yarmo Dru.*[87] *He offered them three settlements in the upper lands: O, Songen and Lowo.*[88] *He offered them three settlements in the centre: Tre, Hlung and Lung.*[89] *He offered them Yarlung*[90] *as a place of residence and Lhasa as a place of practice.*

Thus it is written. [91]

All this came about thanks to the compassionate deeds of Khandro Chöza Bönmo.

Chöza Bönmo's subsequent emanations for the benefit of sentient beings

Once she had achieved the final excellent three bodies, this is how she took rebirth to benefit other sentient beings.

From the mouth of Lama Lishu Tagring:[92]

---

[86] Tib. Za gad ser steng; gTsang po gzhung smad; Chu bar bro sna.
[87] Tib. 'Ol mo lung rung; 'Phan yul 'bram skyes; Yar mo brud.
[88] Tib. 'O; So ngan; Glo bo.
[89] Tib. Pre; sLung; rLung.
[90] Tib. Yar lung Sog kha.
[91] This is clearly recorded in *Tengyur (bsTan 'gyur)*, vol. 182, *Magical Key ('Phrul gyi lde mig)*, an explanatory chapter (bshad byang) from *Dzogchen Yangtse Longchen*, p. 330. This text was written by Khyungpo Lachung Lodrö Gyaltsen (Khyung po Bla chung Blo gros rGyal mtshan) at the Summit Fortress of the White Crystal Crag (Shel gyi brag dkar rtse rdzong), also called Khacho Dragkar (Kha co brag dkar), located to the north of Lake Namtso Chyugmo (gNam mtsho phyug mo). Furthermore, it is said in *The Initiation Instruction (dBang khrid)* that Lama Lishu wrote *The Oral Tradition of Yangtse Longchen (sNyan rgyud yongs rtse klong chen)* at Khacho Dragkar. This was Lishu Tagring's practice place, imbued with his blessings. Yongdzin Rinpoche says that nowadays this mountain is called Sheldrag Ri (Shel brag ri), The Crystal Crag Mountain, and the cave itself is called Sheldrag Phug (Shel brag phug), Crystal Crag Cave.
[92] From *rDzogs pa chen po yongs rtse klong chen, dGongs rgyud drug gi klad don nyi shu rtsa bdun nyams kyi man ngag gnad kyi yig chung*, p. 39, sMad cha (Vol. II), published by Triten Norbutse Library, printed by Si khron mi rigs dpe skrun khang, 2008.

> *"You are the mother of the Buddhas of the three times!*
> *You came into Tibet to benefit beings!*
> *Even though you have departed for the heavenly realm, as the emanation of the Dakini of your body, in the palace of the King of Zahor*[93] *known as Yungdrung Gedenma,*[94] *in the Zhang Zhung city of Deden,*[95] *you will manifest as Dechyo Zangmo.*[96]
> *Between here and Kashmir there will be eighteen such emanations.*
> *As for the emanation of your speech, in central Tibet there will be one called Labdron,*[97] *another called Nyima Dron,*[98] *another called Nyanya,*[99] *and another Kunga Zangmo.*[100] *There will be thirteen such emanations.*
> *As for the emanations of your mind, in Dokham*[101] *in East Tibet there will be one called Zhigmo,*[102] *another called Negugyen,*[103] *and another called Shelza*[104] *who will be a hidden emanation.*
> *In Central Tibet and Samye in particular, your emanations will appear continuously."*

Thus he spoke.

How she manifested the final integration with the Natural State

It was just like this:[105]

> *Chöza Bönmo received the complete instructions on Tantra and Dzogchen from Lama Lishu Tagring*

[93] Tib. Za hor.
[94] Tib. g.Yung drung dGe ldan ma.
[95] Tib. bDe ldan.
[96] Tib. bDe spyod bZang mo.
[97] Tib. Lab sgron.
[98] Tib. Nyi ma sGron.
[99] Tib. Nya nya.
[100] Tib. Kun dga' bZang mo.
[101] Tib. mDo khams.
[102] Tib. Zhig mo.
[103] Tib. Ne gu rgyan.
[104] Tib. Shel za.
[105] Ibid.

and Lachen Drenpa Namkha. She took Dzogchen as her main practice and, integrating everything with this, practised single-mindedly. In one life and in one body, the darkness of the two obscurations was utterly purified into the dimension of the Natural State and Khandro Chöza manifested the ultimate three bodies.

Thus it is said.

In this way, Chöza Bönmo realized the great transfer of the Rainbow Body without manifesting death. But in front of ordinary beings, she kept the appearance of a normal person. Accomplishing inconceivable benefits for the doctrines and for sentient beings, she spontaneously achieved the twofold benefits. Finally, at the age of one hundred and sixty, in a Bönpo cave in Mount Tise,[106] she departed for the heavenly realm of Great Bliss without leaving this body of aggregates behind on earth.

Shenrab Miwo, the great guide of gods and humans,
Who beholds countless beings with his compassion
Entrusted this heart essence which is the doctrine of Sutra, Tantra and Dzogchen
To future generations of sentient beings.

The method to achieve the supreme stage of the three bodies
Is the wish-fulfilling jewel of the excellent path of liberation which is without mistakes or deviations.
As the Liberator of sentient beings, the son of Mu, has said:

"Regarding the support for realizing this path, male and female are equal."

In degenerate times, in the midst of the darkness of samsara,
Like the lamp of existence, the light which clears deep darkness,
You, O Chöza, achieved the pure land of Buddhahood in one lifetime within a body of wisdom, a woman's body.
Departing, you left this story of liberation for us on earth.

[106] Zzng. Ti se - Mt. Kailash.

This hagiography of Chöza Bönmo, the Khandro who achieved the great Rainbow Body in one lifetime and in one body without leaving any remains behind, was extracted for Western students by Nagru Geshe Gelek Jinpa from Dzogchen Dragpa Korsum, Dzogchen Yangtse Longchen, Dzogchen Yetri Thasel, Dzogchen Namkha Truldzö *and* Drangdon Münsel Dronma *as well as many other authentic root texts. It was written in the Western World, in the Bön centre of Shenten Dargye Ling, and was completed on January 15th 2011.*

I have written it according to the needs of our time, compiling it from the essence of many authentic root texts. I confess any errors or mistakes in front of the four objects of refuge. As for whatever merits I may accrue, may they be a cause for the spread of the doctrines and a source of benefit for all sentient beings.

Translated into English by Nagru Geshe Gelek Jinpa, Carol Ermakova and Dmitry Ermakov, Shenten Dargye Ling, Blou, France, March 2011.

མཁའ་འགྲོ་ཙོ་ཟ་བོན་མོའི་རྣམ་ཐར་སྐལ་ལྡན་སེམས་ཀྱི་སྒྲོན་མེ།།

དུས་གསུམ་གདོད་མའི་གཤིས་ལས་མ་གཡོས་བསྟན་འགྲོའི་མགོན་དུ་
མངོན་པར་གར་གྱིས་བཞེངས།།
ཐབས་ཤེས་རོལ་བའི་གསང་ཆེན་རྣལ་འབྱོར་གྲུབ་པའི་ཚོགས་
རྣམས་དགའ་བཞིའི་དཔལ་ལ་བསྙེམས།།
ཉིང་འཛིན་བདེ་བཅུད་ཁོང་དུ་སྨིན་པས་བོན་བརྒྱུད་ཞེན་པ་
དབྱིངས་ཆེན་ངང་དུ་གྲོལ།།
སྣང་བཞི་འོད་གསལ་གཞི་ལ་གོམས་པས་ལྷག་མེད་འཇའ་ལུས་
མངོན་གྱུར་ཙོ་ཟ་བོན་གཅིག་མ།།
སེམས་ཉིད་ལྷ་ཞལ་ཁྲུམས་པས་སྟོང་པ་བློ་ཡིས་རྩིས་གདབ་ཟད།།
དྭངས་མ་ཡེ་ཤེས་རླུང་གིས་ལྷན་སྐྱེས་བདེ་དྲོད་ནང་ནས་ཐར།།
རྩ་གསུམ་འཁོར་ལོ་ལྔ་ཌུ་བཅུ་དྲུག་ཐིག་ལེའི་ཚོམ་བུ་བཀོད།།
དབབ་ལྡོག་འཕྲུལ་གྱིས་ཟུང་འཇུག་བདེ་བའི་ཡེ་ཤེས་མངོན་དུ་གྱུར།།
ཁྱེད་ཀྱི་རྣམ་བཞིའི་འཕྲིན་ལས་ཆ། །ཇི་བཞིན་བརྗོད་པར་མི་ནུས་ཀྱང་། །
དད་ལྡན་ཐར་པར་འཇུག་ངོགས་སུ། །འཆད་ལ་མཁའ་འགྲོས་གནང་བ་སྩོལ། །

ཕྱིར་བདག་ཅག་གི་སྟོན་པ་ཡང་དག་པ་རྫོགས་པའི་སངས་རྒྱས་གཤེན་རབ་མི་བོ་མཆོག་མཐར་ཐུག་སྐུ་གསུམ་གྱི་གོ་འཕང་བརྙེས་པའི་རྗེས་སུ་བསྟན་དང་འགྲོ་བའི་དོན་དུ་ལྷོ་འཛམ་བུ་གླིང་འདིར་སྐུ་སྐྱེ་བ་མི་ཉ་བཞེས་ནས་མདོ་སྔགས་སེམས་གསུམ་གྱི་བསྟན་པ་རྗེས་བཞག་གནང་བ་དང་། བསྟན་པ་དེ་ཉིད་རྗེས་སུ་འཛིན་པའི་འཁོར་ལ་ལྷ་ཀླུ་མི་གསུམ་གྱི་སློབ་མ་བསམ་གྱིས་མི་ཁྱབ་པ་ཡོད་པ་དེ་དག་གིས་སྟོན་པ་དེའི་རྗེས་སུ་བཟུང་ནས་རང་རང་གི་བློ་ཚོད་དང་མཐུན་པའི་བོན་མདོ་སྔགས་སེམས་གསུམ་གྱིས་བསྡུས་པའི་རྒྱལ་བའི་བསྟན་པ་རིན་པོ་ཆེ་འདི་ཉིད་ཉམས་སུ་བླངས་པ་ལ་བརྟེན་ནས་རྣལ་འབྱོར་ཕོ་མོ་དུ་མ་སངས་རྒྱས་པ་དང་། གྲུབ་པ་ཐོབ་པ་བྱུང་བ་ནི་དངོས་ཀྱི་ལོ་རྒྱུས་སྒྲི་ལྟར་ལགས། དམིགས་བསལ་དུ་སངས་རྒྱས་ཀྱི་སྐུ་དུས་སུ་བསྟན་པ་འདིའི་བརྒྱུད་པ་འཛིན་པའི་གཤེན་གྱི་རྣལ་འབྱོར་མ་གཤེན་ཟ་ནེའུ་ཆེན་དང་། གཤེན་ཟ་ནེའུ་ཆུང་། ཀླུ་མོ་མ་མ་དེ་སོགས་མདོ་སྔགས་སེམས་གསུམ་གྱི་བརྒྱུད་པ་འཆང་བའི་གྲུབ་ཐོབ་མ་དུ་མ་ཞིག་བྱོན་ནས་བསྟན་འགྲོར་སྨན་པའི་མཛད་འཕྲིན་བསྐྱངས་མྱོང་ཡོད་ལ། དེ་རྗེས་མདོ་སྔགས་སེམས་གསུམ་གྱིས་བསྡུས་པའི་གཡུང་དྲུང་བོན་གྱི་བསྟན་པ་འདི་ཉིད་འཛམ་གླིང་མཐོ་སྒང་དུ་ཆགས་པའི་

ཤེས་རིག་ཕུན་སུམ་ཚོགས་པའི་ཞིང་ཁམས་ཏེ་ཞང་བོད་ཀྱི་ལྗོངས་འདིར་བསྟན་པ་ཐོག་མར་དར་བས། བོན་བསྟན་སྔ་དར་གྱི་དུས་སུ་གྲུབ་ཐོབ་རྫུ་འཕྲུལ་མ་དགུ་ལ་སོགས་མདོ་སྔགས་སེམས་གསུམ་ལ་གྲུབ་པ་བརྙེས་པའི་གཤེན་གྱི་རྣལ་འབྱོར་མ་དུ་མ་ཞིག་བྱོན་པ་བོན་གྱི་ལོ་རྒྱུས་ཡིག་ཆ་ཁག་ལས་གསལ་བར་འཁོད་ཡོད། བོན་བསྟན་བར་དར་གྱི་མཇུག་དང་། དུས་རབས་བརྒྱད་པའི་ནང་སྐོར་དུ་གཡུང་དྲུང་བོན་གྱི་བསྟན་པའི་སྙིང་པོ་མདོ་སྔགས་རྫོགས་གསུམ་གྱི་གདམས་བརྒྱུད་འཆང་བའི་རྣལ་འབྱོར་མ་དུ་མ་ཞིག་བཞུགས་པའི་ནང་ནས་ཁྱད་པར་འཕགས་པའི་མཐའ་འདུལ་གྱི་བོན་མོ་བཞི་དང་། གྲུབ་ཐོབ་མ་དྲུག་བཅས་བཞུགས་ཡོད་པ་འདི་ལྟར་ཏེ། ཚེ་འདིར་སྐུ་གསུམ་མངོན་དུ་གྱུར་ཅིང་གྲུབ་རྟགས་དང་རྫུ་འཕྲུལ་དཔག་མེད་མངའ་བའི་(1)གཙང་སྟོད་ཀྱི་བོན་མོ་གང་ང་གོང་ཚུང་བྱ་བ་མོན་དང་བོད་ཀྱི་བར་ན་བཞུགས། (2)སྐྱིད་སྨན་གྱི་བོན་མོ་འཁྱོར་ར་འཁྱོར་རྫོང་བྱ་བ་ཧྲན་དྲུག་དང་བོད་ཀྱི་བར་ན་བཞུགས། (3)ཙ་ཟའི་གདང་གྲགས་མ་བྱ་བ་ཞང་ཞུང་དང་བོད་ཀྱི་བར་ན་བཞུགས། (4)མོན་མོ་ཤིབ་ཤིང་གི་དངུལ་མོ་ཆེ་བྱ་བ་རྫ་མི་ཤིང་མི་དང་བོད་ཀྱི་བར་ན་བཞུགས། དེ་བཞི་ནི་ས་མཚམས་སྲུང་བའི་བོན་མོ་བཞི་ཞེས་བྱ་བ་ས་མཚམས་བཞི་ཡི་ཁ་གནོན་དུ་བཞུགས་སོ།།

བོན་མོ་གྲུབ་ཐོབ་མ་དྲུག་ནི། (1)གཤེན་ཟ་མཚོ་སྨན་རྒྱལ་གྱིས་མཚོད་པ་སྤྱི་བོར་བླངས་ནས་གྱེར་བས་ཡེ་ཤེས་ལྷ་རྣམས་ཀྱིས་དངོས་སུ་ལེན་པར་གྲུབ། (2)ཞུ་ཟ་ཛ་ཚུང་རྒྱལ་གྱིས་གང་དུ་འགྲོ་བའི་ས་གནས་ཐུགས་ལ་བཞག་ནས་སྤྱན་བཙུམ་ཞིང་དགོངས་པ་མཛད་པས་ཡུལ་དེར་ཕྱིན་པར་གྲུབ། (3)སྟགས་ཟ་ཧྲི་པང་གིས་ཛ་ལ་ཞོན་ནས་བར་སྣང་དུ་འཕྱོང་ཀྱང་མ་ལྷུང་བར་གྲུབ། (4)ར་ལྷུགས་ཟ་ཡང་རྒྱལ་མས། གཤང་རྟ་ཏུ་ཞོན་ནས་གངས་དཀར་གྱི་རྩེ་ལ་ཉི་མ་འདེ་བར་གྲུབ། (5)སྣ་ནམ་ཟ་བོན་ཚོལ་མས་མཚོ་མ་པང་དར་ཤམ་གཅིག་ཏུ་བཏུམས་ནས་མཚོ་ཐིམ་ཅིང་མི་འབོ་བར་གྲུབ། (6)ཙོ་ཟ་བོན་མོས་ཤ་ཏྲ་སྐམ་པོ་ལ་མདུད་པ་དགུ་མདུད་བྱེད་པར་གྲུབ། དེ་བཞིན་དུ་བོན་མོ་བྱིན་རླབས་ཅན་ཤིན་ཏུ་མང་ངོ་། ཞེས་བསྒྲགས་པ་གླིང་གྲགས་ལས་གསལ།[1] དེའི་ནང་ནས་ལུང་དོན་དང་འབྲེལ་བའི་ལྷག་མེད་འཇའ་ལུས་གཤེགས་པའི་ཙོ་ཟ་བོན་མོའི་རྣམ་ཐར་འཆད་པར་སྤྲོའོ། །དེ་ཡང་ཙོ་ཟ་བོན་མོ་ནི་དུས་རབས་བརྒྱད་པའི་ནང་སྐོར་དུ་ཤིན་ཏུ་སྙན་གྲགས་ཆེ་བའི་བོན་གྱི་རྫོགས་ཆེན་ཉམས་ལེན་གནང་མཁན་ཞིག་དང་། ཁྱད་པར་དུ་བླ་ཆེན་དྲན་པ་ནམ་མཁས་བོན་གྱི་རྫོགས་ཆེན་མོ་རྒྱུད་ཀྱི་གདམས་པ་གཉེར་གཏད་གནང་ས་བོད་ཀྱི་བུ་མེད་ཅིག་ཀྱང་

[1] སོག་སྡེ་སྤྲུལ་སྐུས་དཔར་སྐྲུན་གནང་བའི་བརྗེད་འགྱུར་པོད་72། ལྡེབ་མ་67་ནས་68་བར།

ཡིན། དེ་བཞིན་ཁོང་ནི་བོན་གྱི་རྫོགས་ཆེན་གྱི་བླ་མ་བླ་ཆེན་དྲན་པ་ནམ་མཁའ་དང་། སྔ་ཆེན་ལི་ཤུ་སྟག་རིང་གཉིས་ཀྱི་གསང་ཡུམ་ཡིན་པ་མ་ཟད། སྔགས་རྫོགས་ཟུང་འབྲེལ་གྱི་ཟབ་གདམ་གནང་སའི་སློབ་མ་གཙོ་བོ་ཞིག་ཆགས་ཡོད། དུས་སྐབས་དེར་བླ་ཆེན་དྲན་པ་ནམ་མཁས་བོན་གྱི་རྫོགས་ཆེན་སྙི་རྒྱུད་ཆེན་མོ་ཡེ་ཁྲི་མཐའ་སེལ་དང་། ངེས་དོན་ནམ་མཁའ་འཕྲུལ་མཛོད་ཀྱི་གདམས་སྐོར་རྣམས་བོད་ཁྲི་སྲོང་ལྡེའུ་བཙན་དང་། ལོ་ཆེན་བཻ་རོ་ཙ་ན། མཁའ་འགྲོ་ཚོ་ཟ་བོན་མོ་གསུམ་ལ་གནང་བས། ཚོ་ཟ་བོན་མོ་ནི་བོད་རྒྱལ་ཁྲི་སྲོང་ལྡེའུ་བཙན་དང་ཤིན་ཏུ་ཐུགས་ཡིད་ཟབ་མོ་ཡོད་པའི་གྲོས་ཐུབ་ཀྱི་བོན་གྲོགས་དང་། ཞང་བོད་ལོ་རྒྱུས་ཐོག་འཁོད་པའི་བུད་མེད་ཀྱི་རྟེན་ལ་ཚེ་གཅིག་ལུས་གཅིག་ལ་འཇའ་ལུས་འཕོ་བ་ཆེན་པོའི་སྐུ་བརྙེས་པའི་བོན་མོ་གྲགས་ཅན་ཞིག་ཡིན་པར་གསལ།

སྐུ་སྐྱེ་བ་བཞེས་པའི་སྐོར།

དེ་ཡང་ཚོ་ཟ་བོན་མོ་ནི་ཡུམ་ཆེན་བཟང་ཟ་རིང་བཙུན་གྱི་སྤྲུལ་པ་བསྟན་དང་འགྲོ་བའི་དོན་དུ་ཡུལ་དག་པོ་ཙ་ཤོད་བྱ་བ་ན། ཡབ་ཚོ་ཁྱིམ་བུ་ལན་ཚ་དང་། ཡུམ་བདའ་མོ་ལྕམ་[2]གཉིས་ཀྱི་སྲས་སུ་དུས་རབས་བརྒྱད་པའི་ནང་སྐོར་དུ་འཁྲུངས། མ་ཡི་ཏུམ་ན་ཡོད་པའི་དུས་སུ་སྤྲུལ་པའི་སྐུ་ཡི་རྟགས་སུ་ཏ་དང་ཕཊ་ཀྱི་སྒྲ་སྒྲོགས་པ་དང་། ཡུམ་གྱི་དགོངས་ལམ་དུ་ཉི་མ་ཁོང་ནས་ཤར་བ་སོགས་རྨིས་ལྟས་བཟང་པོ་བྱུང་བ། ཁྱིམ་འཇའ་འོད་ཀྱིས་གང་བ་སོགས་ངོ་མཚར་གྱི་རྟགས་མཚན་དུ་མ་ཤར་རོ།། སྐུ་སྐྱེ་བ་བཞེས་པའི་དུས་སུ་གནོད་སྦྱིན་གྱི་མཁའ་འགྲོ་ཕག་གདོང་མ་དང་། ཤ་ཟན་གྱི་མཁའ་འགྲོ་མ་མང་པོས་བསྐོར་བ་བྱེད་པ། སྔོན་གྱི་ལས་འཕྲོ་བཟང་པོའི་སྟོབས་ཀྱིས་རང་བཞིན་གྱི་ཆགས་པ་ཆུང་ལ་ཤེས་རབ་ཆེ་བ། དགུང་ལོ་ཆེར་སོན་པ་དང་ཡི་གེ་འབྲི་ཀློག་ཀུན་མ་བསླབས་པར་རང་རྩོལ་གྱི་ཚུལ་དུ་མཁྱེན་པ་ཞིག་འཁྲུངས་སོ། །ཚོ་ཟའི་རང་བཞིན་གྱི་མཚན་ཉིད་ནི་སྐྱེ་མཆེད་ལེགས་ལ་ཤེས་རྒྱུད་འཇམ་པ་དང་། མི་ཡི་བུ་མོ་གཞན་དང་མི་འདྲ་བའི་ཁྱད་པར་འཕགས་པའི་རྟགས་བཞི་མངའ་བོ། །དེ་ཡང་ལུས་ལ་པད་མ་དང་མེ་ཏོག་གི་ཚོམ་བུ་ཡོད་པ། ཨ་ཀ་ཏུ་དང་། ཅན་དན་གྱི་དྲི་བྲོ་བ། ཐོ་རངས་དུས་སུ་ནམ་མཁའི་མཐོང་ནས་གཟུགས་མེད་པའི་སྒྲ་སྐད་ཅིག་ཚོ་ཟ་བོན་མོ་ཞེས་ཟེར་གྱིན་འབོད་པ་དང་། རྨི་ལམ་དུ་ལོངས་སྤྱོད་སྣ་ཚོགས་འགྱེད་པ་དང་། ཞང་ཞུང་དང་རྒྱ་གར་གྱི་རིག་འཛིན་གཤེན་པོ་རྣམས་ཀྱིས་དབང་བསྐུར་གདམས་ངག་བཏབ་པ་དང་། ཚོགས་འདྲེན་པ། བྱ་ཁྱུང་ལ་ཞོན་ནས་སུམ་རུ་རྩ་

[2] དྲང་དོན་མུན་སེལ་སྒྲོན་མ་ལས་གཏམ་རྒྱུད་བཛ་ཡི་གཟེར་བུ། ལྡེབ་མ་92་ལས་རྒྱ་མོ་སྐྱིད་ལྕམ་ཞེས་གསལ། ཁྲི་བརྟན་ནོར་བུ་རྩེའི་དཔེ་མཛོད་ཁང་ནས་དཔར་བསྐྲུན་བྱས།

གསུམ་གྱི་ལྷ་གནས་སུ་མཆོད་པ་ལ་ཕྱིན་པ་དང་། ནང་ནུབ་ཀྱི་ལྗོ་དུས་སུ་བྱེའུ་ཚང་ཚོགས་ཀྱི་ཀྲས་དྲན་བསྐུལ་ཚུལ་དུ་སྐད་འབྱིན་པ་སོགས་གསུངས།

༄༅།།གཉེན་གྱི་བླ་མ་དམ་པ་རྣམས་དང་མཇལ་ཚུལ།

དེ་ནས་ཡབ་ཡུམ་གཉིས་ཀྱིས་ཁྱོ་ལ་གཏོང་ཞེས་འཇིག་རྟེན་འཁོར་བའི་ཁྱིམ་ཐབ་བྱེད་པའི་ཆེད་དུ་གསེར་དང་གཡུ་ཡི་རྒྱན་ཆ་སྣ་ཚོགས་བསྒྲུབས་ནས་སྣ་ཚོགས་རྒྱན་གྱིས་སྤྲས་ཏེ་རོལ་རྩེད་ཟླ་ལ་བཏང་ཞེས་གཞོན་ནུའི་གཉེན་སྟོན་གྱི་ཆེད་གྲལ་སྒྲིག་གི་དགའ་སྟོན་ལ་བཏང་བས། འགྲོ་མ་ཉན་པར་གཅིག་པུར་གུད་དུ་བསྡད་པ་ནི་འཁོར་བ་ལ་སྐྱོ་ཤེས་སྐྱེས་ནས་འཇིག་རྟེན་གྱི་སྣང་བ་དང་བློ་མ་འདྲེས་པའི་རྟགས་སོ། །གཤེན་ཚད་མེད་འོད་ལྡན་གྱི་སྤྲུལ་པ་བླ་བོན་དྲན་པ་ནམ་མཁས་ཙོ་ཟ་བོན་མོ་ཉིད་ཡུམ་ཆེན་བཟང་ཟ་རིང་བཙུན་གྱི་སྤྲུལ་པའི་སྐུ་རུ་གཟིགས་ཏེ། བླ་ཆེན་དྲན་པ་ཉིད་སྤྲང་པོ་ཞིག་ཏུ་རྫུས་ནས་ཙོ་ཡི་སྒོ་ཁར་ཕྱིན་ནས་བསོད་སྙོམས་སྟེར་རོགས་ཅེས་བོས་གནང་བས། ཙོ་ཟ་བོན་མོས་གསན་པ་དང་ཕྱུག་ཏུ་མཁར་གཞོང་རྩམ་པས་བཀང་བ་ཞིག་བསྣམས་ནས་སྒོ་ཁར་ཕྱིན་པ་དང་བླ་ཆེན་གྱི་ཞལ་མཇལ་མ་ཐག་ཤིན་ཏུ་སྤྲོ་བ་སྐྱེས་ནས་ལུས་ཀྱི་ཤ་ཞིག་པ་ཙམ་དུ་སོང་ནས་ལུས་འདར་བཞིན་མཁར་གཞོང་དུ་ཞིབ་དྲངས་པས། མཁར་གཞོང་ལག་ནས་ཤོར་ཏེ་ས་ལ་བརྡབས་པས་ཆག་གྲུམ་དུ་སོང་བས་བླ་ཆེན་ལ་འབུལ་རྒྱུའི་རྩམ་ས་ཐོག་ཏུ་འཐོར། དེ་ནས་བླ་ཆེན་དྲན་པས་ཁྱོད་ཀྱིས་མཁར་གཞོང་བཅག་པས་ད་ཁྱོད་ཀྱི་ནོར་ཟས་ཕྱེད་མར་བགོ་དགོས། མི་བགོ་ན་ཁྱོད་ཀྱི་ནོར་བཀུག་པ་ཞིག་ང་ལ་སྤྱིན་དགོས་གསུངས། ཙོ་ཟས་མཁར་གཞོང་བཅག་པ་ཡབ་ཡུམ་གཉིས་ལ་གསང་ནས་ཁྱིམ་ནང་དུ་ཕྱིན་ཏེ་འཇབ་བུས་ཆུ་རིལ་ཞིག་དང་། ཐང་ཞིག་ཁྱུས་ནས་སྒོ་ཕྱིར་ཕྱིན། བླ་མས་ང་ལ་ཅི་ཡོད་གསུངས་པས། ཁྱུས་པའི་དངོས་པོ་དེ་ཉིད་བླ་ཆེན་དྲན་པར་ཕུལ་ནས་བྱིན་རླབས་ཞུས་པས་བླ་མ་ལ་དད་པ་དང་མོས་གུས་གཏིང་ནས་ཆུད། དེ་ནས་ཡབ་ཡུམ་གཉིས་ཀྱིས་བཙ་ཕྱུག་པོ་དང་གཉེན་བསྡེབས་ཀྱི་གྲོས་མོལ་བྱས་པས་འཁོར་བའི་བོན་ལ་སྙིང་པོ་མེད་ཟེར་ནས་བག་མར་མ་ཕྱིན་པའི་ཚུལ་མེད་པ་དང་། སྨྱོན་མའི་སྤྱོད་ཚུལ་མཛད། བག་མ་གཏོང་ཁར་བསམ་ཡས་བྲག་དམར་དུ་བྲོས། གཉེན་འབྲེལ་ཀུན་གྱིས་བཀུགས་ཀྱང་ཁུག་པའི་སྐབས་མེད་པར་དབེན་པའི་གནས་སུ་རྒྱུད་མ་སྨིན་པ་སྨིན་པར་བྱེད་པའི་སྟོན་འགྲོ་བློ་ལྡོག་གི་བོན་ལ་ཐོས་བསམ་སྒོམ་སྒྲུབ་གནང་ནས་བཞུགས་སོ།།

བླ་མེད་རྫོགས་པ་ཆེན་པོའི་དོན་ལ་ཉམས་ལེན་གནང་ཚུལ།

བོན་གྱི་རྫོགས་ཆེན་གྱི་བླ་མ་གཤེན་ཆེན་ལི་ཤུ་སྟག་རིངས་དང་མཇལ་ནས་དེའི་དྲུང་ནས་རྫོགས་ཆེན་བསྒྲགས་པ་སྐོར་གསུམ་དང་། རྫོགས་པ་ཆེན་པོ་ཡང་རྩེ་ཀློང་ཆེན་དྲང་ངེས་ཀྱི་སྐོར་རྣམས་རྫོགས་པར་ཞུས། བླ་མ་ལི་ཤུས་མཁའ་འགྲོ་ཙོ་བྲ་བོན་མོར་མན་ངག་ངོ་སྤྲོད་ཀྱི་གདམས་པ་འདི་ལྟར་བཏབ། རྫོགས་པ་ཆེན་པོ་ཡོངས་རྩེ་ཀློང་ཆེན་ལས་[3]ཡེ་ཤེས་སྤྲུལ་པའི་མཁའ་འགྲོ་ཉོན། །རྒྱལ་ཐེབས་སྤྱི་བླུགས་ལྟ་བའི་དབང་། །རང་བཞིན་ཆ་ལུགས་ཕྱག་རྒྱ་བཅའ། །སྤྱན་རྩ་སེང་གེ་ལྟ་བུ་སྟེ། །རིག་པ་མདུན་གྱི་མཁའ་ལ་གཏད། །རྟོག་མེད་སྤྲོས་བྲལ་བསམ་བརྗོད་བྲལ། །སོ་མ་ལྷུག་པ་མ་བཅོས་པ། །ཀུན་ཏུ་བཟང་པོའི་དགོངས་པ་དེ། །ངོ་སྤྲོད་བྱས་ལ་ངེས་ཤེས་བསྐྱེད། །ཅེས་གསུངས། ཙོ་བྲ་བོན་མོས་བླ་མ་ལི་ཤུས་ཅི་ལྟར་གདམས་པ་བཞིན་ཉམས་སུ་བླངས་པས་བོན་ཉིད་ཀྱི་དགོངས་པ་མངོན་དུ་གྱུར་ནས་ཏས་པོ་རི་རྩེ་མོར་མགུར་འདི་ལྟར་བཞེངས་སོ།།

> [4]ཨེ་མ་ཧོ། ཡ་མཚན་ཆེ། ཉིན་དང་མཚན་མེད་བཞུགས་ཡུལ་ན། །གཏན་དུ་གསལ་བའི་ཉི་མ་ཤར། །དྲོ་ནི་བདག་མོའི་ངོས་ལ་དྲོ། །བོན་དང་སེམས་སུ་སྤྲོད་པས་གཤེན་རབ་དྲིན་པོ་ཆེ། །སེམས་ལ་སེམས་ཀྱིས་ལྟ་བ་རང་ལ་རང་དྲིན་ཆེ། །འཁོར་བའི་གདོས་ཐག་མ་བཅད་ན། །ངས་དང་གནས་སུ་དབང་མེད། །དུག་གསུམ་ཚུ་བོ་མ་བཅད་ན། །ཡེ་ཤེས་མེ་ལ་འབར་དབང་མེད། །འཁོར་བའི་གྲུ་གྲོགས་མ་བསུམ་ན། །བདེ་བའི་རྟ་ལ་རྒྱུགས་དབང་མེད། །བུ་གཉེན་གྲོགས་དང་མ་བྲལ་ན། །རང་སེམས་བྱ་རྒོད་འཕུར་དབང་མེད། །རྣམ་རྟོག་གི་སྡོང་པོ་མ་བཅད་ན། །འཁོར་བའི་ལོ་འདབ་རྒྱས་པར་མཆིས། །དུག་ལྔའི་དགྲ་དང་མ་བྲལ་ན། །འོར་མོ་ཁུང་དུ་འཁྲིད་པར་མཆིས། །གཟུགས་ཕུང་རེ་རྟུལ་མ་བཤིགས་ན། །ཉོན་མོངས་སྐྲུ་དང་བཅས་ནས་མཆིའོ། །ཡེ་ཤེས་མར་མེ་མ་བཏང་ན། །མ་རིག་མུན་པ་སྲོས་པར་མཆིའོ། །ལྟ་བ་རྫོགས་ཆེན་མཁར་ཡོད་པས། །ཉོན་མོངས་དམག་གིས་ང་མི་འཇིགས། །མི་འགྱུར་བརྟན་པའི་གོ་ཡོད་པས། །དུག་ལྔའི་མཚོན་གྱིས་ང་མི་འཇིགས། །ཡེ་ཤེས་སེམས་དཔའི་གྲོགས་ཡོད་པས། །གྲོགས་དང་བྲལ་བས་

---

[3] རྒྱལ་ཐེབས་སྤྱི་བླུགས་ཀྱི་དབང་། ལྡེབ་མ་54། སྨད་ཆ། ཁྲི་བརྟན་ནོར་བུའི་དཔེ་མཛོད་ཁང་གིས་དཔར་སྐྲུན་ཞུས། སི་ཁྲོན་མི་རིགས་དཔེ་སྐྲུན་ཁང་། 2008

[4] རྫོགས་ཆེན་བསྒྲགས་པ་སྐོར་གསུམ། བརྟེན་འགྱུར་སོག་པོད་113། ལྡེབ་མ་256ལས།

ང་མི་འཛིགས། །སེམས་ལ་སྤྱོད་པའི་རྫས་ཡོད་པས། །རྫས་དང་བྲལ་བས་ང་མི་འཛིགས། །ཐམས་ཅད་བྲལ་བས་བདེ་བའི་མཆོག །ཡོངས་དང་བྲལ་བས་བདེ་བའི་མཆོག །གཅིག་པུར་གནས་པས་བདེ་བའི་མཆོག །འཁོར་དང་བྲལ་བས་བདེ་བའི་མཆོག །བོན་དང་སེམས་སུ་སྤྱོད་པ་གཤེན་རབ་དྲིན་པོ་ཆེ། །འཁོར་བའི་འདམ་ལས་སྒྲོལ་བའི་གཤེན་རབ་དྲིན་པོ་ཆེ། །ཉོན་མོངས་རྒྱ་མཚོ་སྐེམས་པའི་གཤེན་རབ་དྲིན་པོ་ཆེ། །སངས་རྒྱས་སེམས་སུ་སྟོན་པའི་གཤེན་རབ་དྲིན་པོ་ཆེ། །རང་སེམས་རང་གིས་རྟོགས་པའི་ཚོ་ཟ་བོན་གཅིག་མ། །ལྟད་མོ་སེམས་ལ་ལྟ་བ་ཡི། །གཏན་གྲོགས་སེམས་ལ་ཚོལ་བ་ཡི། །ཡོངས་སྤྱོད་སེམས་ལ་འཁྱེད་པའི་ཚོ་ཟ་བོན་གཅིག་མ། །ང་ཡི་ལྟ་བ་ནམ་མཁའ་འདྲ། །ང་ཡི་སྤྱོད་པ་ས་གཞི་འདྲ། །ང་ཡི་སྒོམ་པ་ཞུགས་མར་འདྲ། །ང་ཡི་མན་ངག་བདུད་རྩི་འདྲ། །འཁོར་བའི་སེམས་ཅན་ཉོན་མོངས་ཀུན། །རྗེ་དཔོན་འདོད་ན་ཡི་དམ་ལྷ། །གཏན་གྲོགས་འདོད་ན་རང་གི་སེམས། །བྲན་གཡོག་འདོད་ན་བསྟན་སྲུང་ཚོགས། །ཡོངས་སྤྱོད་འདོད་ན་བོན་གྱི་དབྱངས། །ལྟ་ན་རང་གི་སེམས་ལ་ལྟོས། །མཆོད་ན་བདེར་གཤེགས་རིགས་ལྔ་མཆོད། །སྒོམ་ན་མི་རྟོག་ཤེས་རབ་སྒོམས། །འདུག་ན་དགོན་པའི་གནས་སུ་འདུག །ཅེས་ཚོ་ཟ་བོན་མོས་ཧས་པོ་རིའི་རྩེ་མོར་མགུལ་བཞེངས་པའོ། །དེ་ནས་སྒོམ་པ་གླིང་དུ་ཕྱུར་ནས་སངས་རྒྱས་སོ། །ཞེས་གསུངས། ཚོ་ཟས་བླ་ཆེན་དྲན་པ་ནམ་མཁའི་མདུན་ནས་སྤྱི་རྒྱུད་ཆེན་མོ་ཡེ་ཁྲི་མཐའ་སེལ་དང་། རྫོགས་པ་ཆེན་པོ་ནམ་མཁའ་འཕྲུལ་གྱི་མཛོད་ཆེན་གྱི་གདམ་སྐོར། དབང་བཞི་དང་། རིག་པ་རྩལ་དབང་དང་བཅས་པ་རྫོགས་པར་ཉན་ཏེ་རྒྱུད་ལ་སྨིན་གྲོལ་གྱི་དོན་མངའ་བར་མཛད་པ་དང་། ཐོས་བསམ་གྱི་གཙོ་བོ་རྫོགས་ཆེན་བསྒྲགས་པ་སྐོར་གསུམ་ལ་མཛད་ཀྱང་གཞི་ཤར་གྲོལ་རིག་པའི་ཡེ་ཤེས་ཀྱི་སྒྲོང་བ་རྫོགས་ཆེན་ནམ་མཁའ་འཕྲུལ་གྱི་མཛོད་ཆེན་གདམས་སྐོར་ཉམས་སུ་བླངས་པ་ལ་བརྟེན་ནས་རྒྱུད་ལ་སྐྱེས་པར་གསུངས། དེ་ཡང་བླ་ཆེན་དྲན་པ་ནམ་མཁས་ཚོ་ཟ་བོན་མོ་ལ་རྒྱུན་གནས་ཀྱི་མན་ངག་གསུམ་གྱིས་ངོ་སྤྲོད་ཀྱི་གདམས་པ་འདི་ལྟར་བཏབ་སྟེ། ནམ་མཁའ་འཕྲུལ་གྱི་མཛོད་ཆེན་ལས་མན་ངག་གནད་ཀྱི་ལྡེ་མིག་ལས།[5] ཚོ་ཟ་ནམ་མཁའ་ལ་ལྟོས་དང་སྤྲིན་རང་འབྱུང་རང་གྲོལ། ཁར་ཚང་གི་སྤྲིན་དེ་རིང་གི་སྤྲིན་མིན། ད་ཅིའི་སྤྲིན་དེ་ད་ལྟའི་སྤྲིན་མིན། སྤྲིན་སློ་བུར་བ་རང་

[5] ལྡེབ་མ་226། མཛད་པ་པོ་དག་པོའི་དྲན་པ་ནམ་མཁའ། ཁྲི་བརྟན་ནོར་བུ་རྩེའི་དཔེ་མཛོད་ཁང་གིས་དཔར་སྐྲུན་ཞུས།

སར་གྲོལ་བས། སྒྲིབ་བྱེད་ལ་སྙིང་པོ་མེད། ནམ་མཁའ་ཆེན་པོས་སྤྲིན་མ་སྤྱངས། གདོད་ནས་བྲལ་བར་རྒྱུན་དུ་གནས། ཕྱི་ཡི་སྣང་བ་དཀར་དམར་ལ་ལྟོས་དང་། དཔྲ་ཅུ་སྣང་བ་དཔྲ་མིན། གཉེན་དུ་སྣང་བ་གཉེན་མིན། དཔྲ་གཉེན་འཁྲུལ་སྣང་གློ་བུར་བ། སྣང་བ་གློ་བུར་བ་རང་སར་གྲོལ་བས། སྣང་བ་འདི་ལ་སྙིང་པོ་མེད། སྣང་བ་རང་གྲོལ་ཆེན་པོ། འཁྲུལ་སྣང་མ་སྤྱངས་གདོད་ནས་བྲལ་བར་གནས་སོ། །ནང་འཛིན་བྱེད་ཀྱི་ཤེས་པ་སྣ་ཚོགས་སུ་སྣང་བ་ལ་ལྟོས་དང་། དྲན་རྟོག་འཛིན་བྱེད་ཀྱི་ཤེས་པ་གློ་བུར་བ། འཛིན་བྱེད་གློ་བུར་བ་རང་སར་གྲོལ་བས་འཛིན་པ་ལ་དངོས་པོ་མེད། འཛིན་པ་རང་གྲོལ་ཆེན་པོ། འཛིན་རྟོག་མ་སྤྱངས་གདོད་ནས་བྲལ་བར་རྒྱུན་དུ་གནས་ཞེས་སོ། །མེད་པ་གསུམ་ནི། སྐུ་ལས་འདས་པས་ཁ་དོག་དངོས་པོ་མེད། གསུང་ལས་འདས་པས་བརྗོད་བྱ་རྗོད་བྱེད་མེད། ཐུགས་ལས་འདས་པས་གཟུང་ཡུལ་མཚོན་བྱེད་མེད། ཅེས་གདམས་པས། ཙོ་ཟའི་རྒྱུད་ལ་སྙིགས་མ་རྟོག་པའི་བློ་ཡི་དྲི་མ་ཐམས་ཅད་འཛིན་མེད་རང་གྲོལ་ཆེན་པོའི་ངང་དུ་གྲོལ་སྟེ་རང་རིག་ཡེ་ཤེས་རྗེན་གཅེར་དུ་ཤར་བའོ། །དེ་ནས་ཧས་པོ་རི་ལ་སྒོམ་སྒྲུབ་མཛད་པས་མཆོག་དང་ཐུན་མོང་གི་དངོས་གྲུབ་རྒྱུད་ལ་བརྙེས་པས་རྫུ་འཕྲུལ་ཞབས་ཀྱིས་ཧས་པོ་རི་ལ་གོམ་པ་གསུམ་གྱིས་ཕྱིན་པ་དང་། ཤ་ཅུ་སྐམ་པོ་ལ་མདུད་པ་དགུ་མདུད་བྱེད་པར་གྲུབ། ཏིང་ངེ་འཛིན་གྱི་རྩལ་གྱིས་བླ་མ་སྤྱན་འདྲོངས་ནུས་པ། འཇིག་རྟེན་ཁམས་ཀྱི་ཟས་སྤངས་ནས་ཏིང་ངེ་འཛིན་གྱི་བཅུད་ལ་རོལ་སྟེ་བླ་མེད་རྫོགས་པ་ཆེན་པོའི་དོན་ཉམས་སུ་ལེན་བཞིན་བཞུགས་སོ། །སྐབས་དེར་ཙོ་ཟའི་རྒྱུད་ལ་མ་གཞི་ཇི་བཞིན་ཉིད་ཀྱི་སྐྱེ་མཆེད་མངོན་དུ་གྱུར་ནས་བུ་རྩལ་ཤར་རིག་པའི་ཡེ་ཤེས་དང་འདུ་འབྲལ་མེད་པ་ཡིན་ཀྱང་ལམ་ཁྲིགས་ཆོད་ཀྱི་ཉམས་ལེན་གོམས་པ་ཚད་དུ་ཕྱིན་པ་དང་། ལྷུན་གྲུབ་འོད་གསལ་གྱི་སྣང་བ་རྒྱ་རལ་བའི་ཆེད་དུ་མུན་པའི་རྣལ་འབྱོར་ལ་བཞུགས་ནས་བླ་མེད་རྫོགས་པ་ཆེན་པོའི་དོན་ཉམས་སུ་བླངས་ཡོད་པ་ནི། བླ་མ་ལི་ཤུས་ཙོ་ཟ་ལ་གདམས་པ། རྫོགས་པ་ཆེན་པོ་ཡོངས་རྫེ་སྙིང་ཆེན་ལས།[6] འོད་གསལ་གཞི་སྒྱུར་གདམས་པ་འདི། །སངས་རྒྱས་བཙན་ཐབས་སྒྲུབ་པའི་མན་ངག་ཡིན། །མུན་པའི་སྙིང་ནས་སྣང་བའི་འོད། །ཡེ་ཤེས་ཆེན་པོའི་རང་དྭངས་འཆར། །གོམས་ཤིང་འདྲིས་པར་བྱས་པ་ན། །སངས་རྒྱས་ཉེ་བར་སྒྲུབ་མི་དགོས།

[6] རྒྱལ་ཐེབས་དབང་ཁྲིད་གནད་ཀྱི་ལག་ལེན་ལྡེབ་མ་146། སྨད་ཆ། ཁྲི་བརྟན་ནོར་རྩེའི་དཔེ་མཛོད་ཁང་གིས་དཔར་སྐྲུན་ཞུས། སི་ཁྲོན་མི་རིགས་དཔེ་སྐྲུན་ཁང་། 2008

།ཅེས་སོ། ཚོ་ཟླས་དེ་ལྟར་ཉམས་སུ་བླངས་པས་ལམ་ཁྲིགས་ཆོད་ཀྱི་ཉམས་ལེན་གོམས་པ་རླུང་དུ་གྱུར་པའོ། །དེ་ནས་ཚོ་ཟླ་བོན་མོས་བླ་མ་སྣ་ཆེན་ལི་ཤུ་སྟག་རིང་གི་མདུན་ནས་ལྷུན་གྲུབ་འོད་གསལ་ཐོད་རྒལ་གྱི་ཉམས་ལེན་སྐོར་གྱི་ཟབ་གདམ་རྣམས་ཞུས་ནས་ཉམས་སུ་བླངས་པས་མཐར་ཐུག་སྣང་བཞི་ཟད་སར་ཕྱིན་ནས་འཇའ་ལུས་འཕོ་བ་ཆེན་པོའི་གོ་འཕང་བརྙེས་པའོ། །དེ་ཡང་། རྫོགས་པ་ཆེན་པོ་ཡང་རྩེ་ཀློང་ཆེན་ལས་དགོངས་རྒྱུད་དྲུག་གི་ཀླད་དོན་ཉི་ཤུ་རྩ་བདུན་ཉམས་ཀྱི་མན་ངག་གནད་ཀྱི་ཡིག་ཆུང་ལས།[7] ཡེ་ཤེས་སྤྲུལ་པའི་མཁའ་འགྲོ་མ། །འཕྲུལ་པའི་སྣང་བ་ཞིང་ལྟས་སྦྱངས། །ཕུང་པོའི་གདོས་པ་ལྷ་ལྟས་བཀོལ། །ཤེས་པའི་མཚན་མ་འོད་ལྟས་དྲིལ། །དོན་དུ་ཡེ་ཤེས་ལྟ་ལ་བཟླ། །སྒྲ་འོད་ཟེར་གསུམ་འཕྲུལ་སྣང་གསུམ། །སྐུ་གསུམ་སེམས་སུ་དམར་ཐག་བཅད། །ཆོ་འདིར་གོམས་འདྲིས་སེམས་ལ་བྱ། །ནང་དྲོད་རྟགས་ཉག་ཐག་ཐིག་ལེ་དང་། །ཡིག་འབྲུ་ལྷ་སྐུ་ཞིང་ཁམས་འཆར། །སྒྱུ་ལུས་འབྱུང་ལྔ་འཇིག་དུས་སུ། །འབྱུང་ལྔའི་གཡར་པོ་རང་སར་བཞག །འོད་ལྔའི་དྭངས་མ་ལྷ་ལྔ་དང་། །སེམས་ཉིད་རང་དྭངས་བླང་དོར་བྲལ། །དབུ་མའི་ལམ་ལ་རིག་པ་ཧཱུྃ། །འོད་ལྔའི་ཉག་ཐག་ཐབས་ཀྱིས་དྲངས། །ཀུན་ཏུ་བཟང་པོའི་ཐུགས་ཁའི་གཡུང་དྲུང་ལ། །སྒྲ་འོད་ཟེར་གསུམ་གཅིག་ཏུ་དྲིལ། །ཡེ་ཤེས་ཟང་ཐལ་མངོན་སངས་རྒྱས། །ཅེས་གདམས་པ་བཞིན་ཚོ་ཟླས་ཉམས་སུ་བླངས་པས་སྒྱུ་ལུས་གདོས་བཅས་ཀྱི་ཕུང་པོ་དང་། ཐལ་མལ་གྱི་སྣང་བ་སྒྲ་རག་དང་བཅས་པ་ཐམས་ཅད་གཞི་ཡང་མེས་ཆེན་པོ་ངོ་བོ་ཉིད་ཀྱི་ཀློང་དུ་ཁྲོལ་གྱིས་གྲོལ་ནས་ཟག་མེད་ཡེ་ཤེས་ཀྱི་སྐུ་མཆོག་མངོན་དུ་བྱས་པའོ།།

བསྟན་འགྲོའི་དོན་ཆེན་མཛད་པའི་སྐོར།

བོད་རྒྱལ་ཐོག་མ་གཉའ་ཁྲི་བཙན་པོ་ནས་བཟུང་བོད་རྒྱལ་ཁྲི་སྲོང་ལྡེའུ་བཙན་བར་དུས་སྐབས་རེ་ཙམ་བོན་བསྟན་ཅུང་ཙམ་འཕེལ་འགྲིབ་ཕྱིན་ཡོད་ནའང་གཙོ་བོའི་ཆ་ནས་བོད་གངས་ཅན་གྱི་ལྗོངས་འདིར་བོན་བསྟན་དར་ཞིང་རྒྱས་པ་གྱུར། བོད་རྒྱལ་ཁྲི་སྲོང་ཡང་སྐུ་ཚེ་སྟོད་དུ་གཡུང་དྲུང་བོན་གྱི་སྐོར་ཞུགས་ནས་བོན་གྱི་རྫོགས་ཆེན་གྱི་བླ་མ་དྲན་པ་ནམ་མཁའི་དྲུང་ནས་རྫོགས་པ་ཆེན་པོ་ནམ་མཁའ་འཕྲུལ་གྱི་མཛོད་ཆེན་དྲང་ངེས་སྐོར་གྱི་ཁྲིད་གདམས་ཞུས་ནས་བོན་བསྟན་ལ་ཉམས་ལེན་གནང་བའི་

[7] ལྡེབ་མ་28། སྨད་ཆ། ཁྲི་བརྟན་ནོར་རྩེའི་དཔེ་མཛོད་ཁང་གིས་དཔར་སྐྲུན་ཞུས། སི་ཁྲོན་མི་རིགས་དཔེ་སྐྲུན་ཁང་། 2008

ཚུལ་བོན་གྱི་ལོ་རྒྱུས་ཡིག་ཆ་རྣམས་སུ་གསལ་བར་འཁོད་ཡོད། དེ་ཡང་དྲང་དོན་ལུན་སེལ་སྒྲོན་མ་ལས།[8] ཐུགས་ཀྱི་བརྟག་པ་སྐན་རྒྱུད་རྣམ་པ་གཉིས། །མངའ་བསྙེམས་དུས་ལ་འཛོམས་པའི་རིགས་ཅན་ལྷ་ལ་གནང་། །བཻ་རོ་ཙ་ན་མངའ་བདག་རྒྱལ་པོ་དང་། །ཙོ་ཟ་བོན་མོ་གསུམ་ནི་མཆོག་ཐོབ་མངོན་སངས་རྒྱས། ཅེས་གསུངས། རྒྱ་མཚན་འདི་འདྲ་ཞིག་ལ་བརྟེན་ནས་བོན་གྱི་ལོ་རྒྱུས་ཡིག་ཆ་ཁག་ལས་བོད་རྒྱལ་ཁྲི་སྲོང་ལྡེའུ་བཙན་ལ་འགྲེལ་བཤད་བྱེད་ཚུལ་མི་འདྲ་བ་གཉིས་བྱུང་ཡོད་པ་དེ་ནི་རྟ་བའི་ཆོས་ལུགས་ཀྱི་འདུ་ཤེས་འཛིན་ཚུལ་ལ་བརྟེན་ནས་བྱུང་ཡོད་པར་སེམས། དཔེར་ན་བོད་ཀྱི་བན་དེ་ཆོས་རྒྱ་གར་ནང་ཆོས་བོད་ལ་དར་བར་འགོག་རྐྱེན་བྱེད་པའི་བོད་ཀྱི་རྒྱལ་པོ་ལྷ་སྲས་དར་མ་དང་། བོན་པོ་ཡིན་པའི་བོད་ཀྱི་བློན་པོ་རྣམས་ལ་བདུད་རྒྱལ་དང་བདུད་བློན་ཞེས་པའི་ཐ་སྙད་བྱེད་པ་ནང་བཞིན་བོན་པོའི་དཔེ་ཆ་འགའ་ཞིག་ནས་ཁྲི་སྲོང་ལྡེའུ་བཙན་གྱིས་བོན་ཆོས་ཉམས་སུ་བླངས་པའི་རྒྱུ་མཚན་གྱིས་བདེར་གཤེགས་སྤྲུལ་པ་དང་། བོན་བསྟན་བསྣུམས་པས་ཆ་ནས་བདུད་དང་རྒྱལ་འགོང་སོགས་ཀྱི་བྱིན་རླབས་ཞུགས་པར་བཤད་ཡོད། བོད་རྒྱལ་ཁྲི་སྲོང་ལྡེའུ་བཙན་དགུང་ལོ་ཆེར་སོན་པ་དང་སློབ་དཔོན་པད་མ་འབྱུང་གནས་དང་། མཁན་པོ་ཤནྟི་ར་ཀྵི་གཉིས་གཙོས་པའི་རྒྱ་གར་དང་། རྒྱ་ནག་ཕྱོགས་ནས་ཕེབས་པའི་ཆོས་བླ་རྣམས་དང་། བོད་ཀྱི་ཆོས་བློན་ཚོའི་རེ་འདོད་དང་བསྟུན་ནས་རྒྱལ་པོས་གཡུང་དྲུང་བོན་གྱི་བསྟན་པ་སྣུབ་པའི་དུས་སུ་བོད་མི་རང་གིས་བོད་རང་སར་རིག་གནས་གསར་བརྗེའི་ལས་འགུལ་སྤེལ་བ་དང་། བོད་རང་ས་ནས་བྱུང་བའི་ཐུན་མོང་མ་ཡིན་པའི་ཆོས་ལུགས་ཏེ་མདོ་སྔགས་སེམས་གསུམ་གྱིས་བརྒྱུས་པའི་གཡུང་དྲུང་བོན་གྱི་གསུང་རབ་དུ་མ་ཞིག་མེར་བསྲེགས་པ་དང་། ཆུ་དང་རླུང་ལ་བསྐུར་བ། བོན་གྱི་དགོན་སྡེ་དང་སྐུ་གསུང་ཐུགས་རྟེན་རྣམས་གཏོར་བཤིགས་བཏང་བ་མ་ཟད། བོན་གྱི་བླ་མ་དང་། བོན་གྱི་བློན་པོ། བོན་གྱི་མི་དྲག བོན་གྱི་མི་མང་དུ་མ་ཞིག་དམར་གསོད་བཏང་བ་དང་། མཐའ་འབུད་བཏང་བ། ལོངས་སྤྱོད་གཞུང་བཞེས་བྱས་པ། ཆོས་ལུགས་བསྒྱུར་བ་སོགས་ཡ་ངལ་བའི་ལས་སྤྱོད་ཅི་རིགས་སུ་སྤེལ་བས་བོད་ཀྱི་དབུས་སྐོར་དུ་ཙོ་ཟ་བོན་མོ་མ་གཏོགས་བོན་ཆོས་གཙང་མར་སྤྱོད་པའི་བོན་པོ་མེད་པར་གྱུར། བོད་རྒྱལ་ཁྲི་སྲོང་གིས་བོན་བསྟན་བསྣུབས་པའི་དུས་སུ་བོན་གཤེན་རིག་འཛིན་མཁའ་འགྲོ་རྣམས་ཀྱིས་བཀའ་བསྒྲོས་མཛད་དེ་བོན་གྱི་གསུང་རབ་ཧྲེ་སྙེད་ཅིག་ཟབ་གཏེར་དུ་སྦས་པ་དང་། སྤྲས་འཕྲོ་རྣམས་འགའ་ཞིག་ཆོས་སུ་བསྒྱུར་བ་དང་། ཆོས་དང་འདྲ་མཚུངས་སུ་བཅོས་པ་སོགས་བྱས་པས་ཕྱིས་སུ་གཏེར་མ་དང་། སྐན་རྒྱུད། བོན་པོ་གསར་མའི་ལུགས་སྲོལ་སོགས་བྱུང་ཡོད་པ་རེད། ཙོ་ཟ་

[8] ལྡེབ་མ་32་ནས། ཁྲི་བརྟན་ནོར་བུ་རྩེའི་དཔེ་མཛོད་ཁང་ནས་དཔར།

བོན་མོ་བོད་རྒྱལ་ཁྲི་སྲོང་ལྡེའུ་བཙན་གྱི་མཆེད་གྲོགས་ཡིན་པས་རྒྱུ་མཚན་ནམ། ཡང་ན་མཐུ་རྩལ་དང་རྫུ་འཕྲུལ་ཆེ་བའམ། འཇིག་རྟེན་བློས་བཏང་ནས་ཚེ་གཅིག་དབེན་པའི་གནས་སུ་སྒོམ་སྒྲུབ་གནང་ནས་བཞུགས་པའི་རྒྱུ་མཚན་བཅས་གང་ཡིན་ཡང་དུས་ཀྱི་གཉན་འཕྲང་དེ་ལྟ་བུའི་འོག་ཅོ་ཟ་བོན་མོ་ཉིད་བོད་དབུས་སུ་གཡུང་དྲུང་བོན་ཉམས་སུ་ལེན་བཞིན་བཞུགས་རྒྱུ་བྱུང་བ་ཤིན་ཏུ་ངོ་མཚར་ཆེའོ། །སྐབས་དེར་བོད་དུ་མི་བདེ་བ་སྣ་ཚོགས་བྱུང་བས། ཅོ་ཟ་བོན་མོ་མཁར་ཆེན་བྲག་དཀར་ལ་[9]བཞུགས་པ་ལ་རྒྱལ་པོས་མི་བདེ་སྣ་ཚོགས་བྱུང་བ་འདི་རྣམས་རྟོས་ཅིས་ལེན་ཞུས་པས། བོན་མོ་ན་རེ། རྒྱལ་པོ་ཁྱེད་ཀྱིས་ཅི་ཡང་བྱེད། ཡ་བོ་མི་བྱེད་པ་ལ་བྱས། བཀྲ་ཤིས་ཀྱི་བོན་བསྣུབས། བོན་པོ་རྣམས་མཐའ་རུ་སྤྱུགས་པ་དང་བོན་སྤྱངས་པས་ལེན། ད་ཡང་ལོ་གསུམ་ཚུན་ཆད་ལ། རྒྱལ་སྲིད་རྩེད་ནས་མི་ཆགས་ཟེར། དེ་ལ་ཅི་བྱས་ན་ཕན་ཞུས་པས། གཤེན་པོ་རྣམས་ཐམས་ཅད་གདན་འདྲེན་ཞུ་ནས་བོན་སྤྱོད་དུ་བཙུག རྒྱལ་བློན་གྱིས་མགུར་ལྷ་དང་ཕོ་ལྷ་ལ་སྐྱབས། སེལ་དང་བསང་མཆོད་སྣང་སྲིད་ཞི་བ་ཆེན་པོ་བྱས་ན་ཕན་ཟེར་རོ། །དེ་ནས་རྒྱལ་པོས་བདེན་པར་གོ་སྟེ་གཤེན་པོ་རྣམས་གདན་འདྲེན་ཅི་ལྟར་བྱེད་པར་གྲོས་པས། ལ་ལ་ན་རེ་བོན་གཤེན་རྣམས་བྱང་མྱུ་ངམས་སུ་གྲོངས་ནས་མེད་ཟེར་རོ། །ཅོ་ཟས་གཤེན་པོ་རྣམས་བྱང་སྤང་གོང་གི་ཁྲིམ་ན་བྲག་སྲིན་མིག་དམར་འཕོལ་པོ་བྱས། རི་དྭགས་སྤྱུ་སྤྱུག་གི་འོ་མ་འཇོ་ཡིན་ཡོད། གཤེན་པོ་རྣམས་ཀྱིས་གསུངས་པ་ལ་ཉན་ཅིང་། ཆེ་གེ་ཡིག་ཚང་སྟེར་ན་ངས་གདན་འདྲེན་གསུངས་པས། བོད་རྒྱལ་ཁྲི་སྲོང་གིས་དེ་ལྟར་འཐད་པ་ཞལ་བཞེས་གནང་བ་དང་། རྒྱལ་པོས་འོ་ན་བོན་གཤེན་རྣམས་གདན་དྲངས་འཚལ་ཞུས་ཏེ་གསེར་དངུལ་བྱ་བོ་གང་ཕུལ་བས། ཅོ་ཟ་བོན་མོས་དྲེའུ་འཕར་མ་དཀྱུ་རྐང་ཞིག་བཅིབས་ནས་ལྷོང་ལྷ་གསོལ་གྱིན་བྱོན་པས་གཤེན་པོ་རྣམས་དང་མཇལ་ནས་བོད་དུ་མི་བདེ་བ་སྣ་ཚོགས་བྱུང་ནས་གཤེན་པོ་རྣམས་སྤྱན་འདྲེན་དུ་མཆིས་པས་གཤེགས་འཚལ་ཞུས་པས། མི་ཉག་ཟླེ་ཚ་མཁར་བུས་ན་རེ། བོན་ལ་འགྲོ་དོན་ལས་མེད། སེམས་ཅན་ལ་སྙིང་རྗེ་བས་འགྲོ་གསུངས་ནས་གཤེན་པོ་རྣམས་བྱོན་ནོ། །དེ་ནས་ཕོ་བྲང་དུ་ཕེབས་ཏེ་རྒྱལ་པོ་དང་ཞེ་ས་རྩེ་སྤྲོད་དུ་མཛད་དོ། །གཤེན་པོ་རྣམས་ཀྱིས་དང་པོར་རྒྱལ་

---

[9]བརྟེན་འགྱུར་པོད་182རྫོགས་ཆེན་ཡོངས་རྩེའི་བཤད་བྱང་འཕྲུལ་གྱི་ལྡེ་མིག་ལྡེབ་མ་330་ལས་གསལ་བ་འདི་ལྟར། ཤེལ་གྱི་བྲག་དཀར་རྩེ་རྫོང་ནི། ཁ་ཅོ་བྲག་དཀར་ཡང་ཟེར་སྟེ། གནམ་མཚོ་ཕྱུག་མོའི་བྱང་ཕྱོགས་ན་ཡོད་དོ། ཁྱུང་པོ་བླ་ཆུང་བློ་གྲོས་རྒྱལ་མཚན་གྱིས་མཛད་པའོ། །དབང་ཁྲིད་ལས། ཁ་ཅོ་བྲག་དཀར་དུ་བླ་མས་སྙན་རྒྱུད་ཡོངས་རྩེ་ཀློང་ཆེན་མཛད་ཅེས་པའོ། །དེ་ནི་བླ་མ་ལི་ཤུ་སྟག་རིང་གི་སྒྲུབ་གནས་བྱིན་ཅན་དང་དེང་སང་རི་བོ་དེ་ལ་ཤེལ་བྲག་རི་དང་ཕུག་པ་ལ་ཤེལ་བྲག་ཕུག་ཅེས་འབོད་པ་ཡོངས་འཛིན་སྨྲ་བའི་དབང་པོས་གསུངས།

འགོང་གི་ཁ་གཉན་དུ་གསས་ཁང་ཞིག་བཞེངས་དགོས་གསུངས་ནས་པེ་དཀར་གླིང་དུ་གསས་ཁང་ཞིག་བཞེངས། མཆོད་རྟེན་ནག་པོ་བོན་ལུགས་སུ་བཞེངས་སོ། །བོན་གཤེན་རྣམས་ཀྱིས་གཏོ་བཅོས་མཛད་པ་དང་། རྒྱལ་བློན་རྣམས་ཀྱིས་རྗེ་ཡི་མགུར་ལྷ་གསོལ་བ་དང་ཕོ་ལྷར་སྐྱབས་སུ་གསོལ་བས། ལྷ་ཞལ་ཚུར་གཟིགས། ཡར་ཆབ་རྣལ་དུ་ཕབ། དྲན་པ་ནམ་མཁའ་ནན་བན་ནས་བཏོན་ཏེ་རྗེ་ལ་ཆོ་དབང་བསྐུར་བས་རྒྱལ་པོ་སྣང་བ་དྭངས། བོད་ཁམས་སུ་ནད་རིགས་དང་འབྲུགས་པ་ཆད་པས། རྒྱལ་པོ་དགྱེས་ཏེ་བོན་ལ་ཆེ་ཐབས་ཡིག་ཚང་ཕུལ་བ་ནི། སྟོད་ནས་ཡུལ་གསུམ་ཕུལ་བ་ནི་ཟ་གད་སེར་སྟེང་། གཙང་པོ་གཞུང་སྨད། ཚ་བར་ཐོ་སྣ་དང་གསུམ་མོ། །སྨད་ནས་ཡུལ་གསུམ་ཕུལ་ཏེ། འོལ་མོ་ལུང་རུང་དང་། འཕན་ཡུལ་འབྲམ་སྐྱེས། ཡར་མོ་བྲུད་དང་གསུམ་མོ། །སྟོད་ནས་འབང་གསུམ་ཕུལ་ཏེ་འོ་དང་། སོ་ངན། ཤྲོ་བོ་གསུམ་མོ། །དབུས་ནས་འབངས་གསུམ་ཕུལ་ཏེ། པྲེ། སྨུང་། ཀླུང་གསུམ་མོ། །ཡར་ལུང་སོག་ཁ་བཞུགས་པའི་གནས་སུ་ཕུལ། ལྷ་ས་ཐུགས་དམ་གྱི་ལྷ་གསོལ་བའི་གནས་སུ་ཕུལ་ལོ། །ཞེས་བསྒྲགས་པ་གླིང་གྲགས།[10] དེ་ནི་མཁའ་འགྲོ་ཙོ་ཟ་བོན་མོའི་ཐུགས་རྗེའི་མཛད་འཕྲིན་ལ་བརྟེན་ནས་བྱུང་བ་ཡིན་ནོ།།

གདུལ་བྱ་གཞན་དོན་དུ་སྤྲུལ་སྐུ་བྱོན་ཚུལ།

ཙོ་ཟ་བོན་མོ་མཆོག་མཐར་ཐུག་སྐུ་གསུམ་གྱི་གོ་འཕང་བརྙེས་ནས་གདུལ་བྱ་གཞན་དོན་དུ་སྐྱེ་བ་བཞེས་ཚུལ་ནི་ཡང་རྩེ་ཀློང་ཆེན་དགོངས་རྒྱུད་དྲུག་གི་ཀློང་དོན་39ལས། བླ་མའི་ཞལ་ནས། ཁྱོད་ནི་དུས་གསུམ་སངས་རྒྱས་འབྱུང་བའི་ཡུམ། །བོད་དུ་འགྲོ་བའི་དོན་ལ་བྱོན། །མཁའ་སྤྱོད་གནས་སུ་གཤེགས་གྱུར་ཀྱང་། ཁྱོད་ཀྱི་སྐུ་ལས་སྤྲུལ་པའི་མཁའ་འགྲོ་ནི། །ཟ་ཧོར་རྒྱལ་པོའི་ཕོ་བྲང་དུ། །གཡུང་དྲུང་དགེ་ལྡན་མ་བྱ་བ་དང་། །ཞང་ཞུང་གྲོང་ཁྱེར་བདེ་ལྡན་དྲུང་། །བདེ་སྐྱིད་བཟང་མོ་བྱ་བ་དང་། ཁ་ཆེ་ཡན་ལ་བཅོ་བརྒྱད་འབྱུང་། །གསུང་གི་སྤྲུལ་པ་ལས། དབུས་སུ་ལབ་སྒྲོན་བྱ་བ་དང་། །ཉི་མ་སྒྲོན་དང་ཉ་ཉ་དང་། །ཀུན་དགའ་བཟང་མོ་བྱ་བ་དང་བཅུ་གསུམ་ཡོད་། ཐུགས་ཀྱི་སྤྲུལ་པ་ལས། མདོ་ཁམས་ཞིག་མོ་བྱ་བ་དང་། །ནེ་གུ་རྒྱན་ཞེས་བྱ་བ་དང་། །ཞིལ་ཟ་བྱ་བའི་བུད་མེད་ཡོད་། །སྨྲས་པའི་ཚུལ་ཅན་ཞིག་འབྱུང་གསུངས། ཁྱད་པར་དབུས་དང་བསམ་ཡས་སུ། ཁྱོད་ཀྱི་སྤྲུལ་པ་རེ་རེ་ཡོད་། ཞེས་གསུངས་སོ།།

[10] ལྡེབ་མ་91་ནས་93་བར་གསལ།

ཐ་མ་དབྱིངས་སུ་གཤེགས་ཚུལ།

དེ་ལྟར་ཙོ་ཟ་བོན་མོས་བླ་མ་ཡི་ཤུ་སྟག་རིང་དང་། བླ་ཆེན་དྲན་པ་ནམ་མཁའ་སོགས་ཀྱི་མདུན་ནས་ཐུགས་སེམས་ཀྱི་གདམ་པ་རྫོགས་པར་ཞུས་ནས་བླ་མེད་རྫོགས་པ་ཆེན་པོའི་དོན་ལ་རྒྱང་དེད་ཆིག་དྲིལ་དུ་ཉམས་སུ་བླངས་པས་ཚེ་གཅིག་ལུས་གཅིག་ལ་སྒྲིབ་གཉིས་མུན་པའི་ཚོགས་རྣམས་དབྱིངས་སུ་སངས་ཏེ་མཐར་ཐུག་སྐུ་གསུམ་གྱི་གོ་འཕང་མངོན་དུ་བྱས་པ་གསུངས། དེ་ལྟར་སྐུ་ཚེའི་འདུ་བྱེད་མ་བོར་བར་འཇའ་ལུས་འཕོ་བ་ཆེན་པོ་མངོན་དུ་བྱས་ཀྱང་གདུལ་བྱ་ཐུན་མོང་གི་སྣང་ངོར་ཐ་མལ་གྱི་ཚུལ་བཟུང་ནས་བསྟན་དང་འགྲོ་བའི་དོན་ཆེན་བསམ་གྱིས་མི་ཁྱབ་པར་མཛད་པས་དོན་གཉིས་ལྷུན་གྱིས་གྲུབ་པའོ། །མཐར་དགུང་ལོ་བརྒྱ་དང་དྲུག་བཅུ་བཞེས་པ་དང་ཧི་སེའི་བོན་ཕུག་ཏུ་ཕུང་པོ་ས་ལ་མ་བཞག་པར་མཁའ་སྤྱོད་བདེ་བ་ཆེན་པོའི་ཞིང་ཁམས་སུ་གཤེགས་སོ།།

ལྷ་མིའི་རྣམ་འདྲེན་གཤེན་རབ་མི་བོ་ཡིས།
།མཐའ་ཡས་འགྲོ་ལ་བརྩེ་བས་ཉེར་གཟིགས་ནས། །
ཐུགས་ཀྱི་ཉིང་ཁུ་མདོ་ཐུགས་སེམས་ཀྱི་བོན།
།ཕྱི་རབས་འགྲོ་བའི་དོན་དུ་གཉེར་གཏད་མཛད། །

ཡང་དག་སྐུ་གསུམ་གོ་འཕང་བརྙེས་པའི་ཐབས།
།གོལ་དང་འཆུག་མེད་ལམ་མཆོག་ཡིད་བཞིན་ནོར། །
ཐོབ་པའི་རྟེན་ལ་ཕོ་མོ་ཁྱད་མེད་པར།
།དམུ་སྲས་འགྲོ་བའི་མགོན་པོའི་ཞལ་བཞེས་བཞིན།
དུས་ཀྱི་སྙིགས་མ་འཁོར་བའི་མུན་ཁྲོད་དུ།
།སྲིད་པའི་སྒྲོན་མེ་སྣང་རིམ་སེལ་བའི་འོད། །
ཤེས་རབ་རྟེན་ལ་ཚེ་ཆིག་སངས་རྒྱས་སར།
།གཤེགས་པའི་རྣམ་ཐར་ཁྱེད་ཀྱིས་ཞིང་འདིར་བཞག།
ཚུལ་འདི་དུས་དང་དགོས་པའི་སྐབས་བསྟུན་ཏེ།
།གཞུང་བཟང་དུ་མའི་བཅུད་ཕྱུང་ཟུར་དུ་བཀོད། །
འགལ་འཁྲུལ་གནས་བཞིར་བཤགས་ཤིང་རྣམ་དཀར་ཆ།
།ཇི་མཆིས་བསྟན་འགྲོར་སྨན་པའི་རྒྱུར་གྱུར་ཅིག །

ཅེས་ཚེ་གཅིག་ལུས་གཅིག་ལ་ལྷག་མེད་འཇའ་ལུས་སུ་གཤེགས་པའི་མཁའ་འགྲོ་ཙོ་ཟ་བོན་མོའི་རྣམ་ཐར་འདི་ཉིད་རྫོགས་ཆེན་བསྙགས་པ་སྐོར་གསུམ་དང་། རྫོགས་ཆེན་ཡོངས་རྩེ་ཀློང་ཆེན། རྫོགས་ཆེན་ཡེ་ཁྲི་མཐའ་སེལ། རྫོགས་ཆེན་ནམ་མཁའ་འཕྲུལ་མཛོད། དྲང་དོན་མུན་སེལ་སྒྲོན་མ་སོགས་རང་གཞུང་ཁུངས་མ་དུ་མར་གཏུགས་ནས་ནག་ཏུ་དགེ་བཤེས་དགེ་ལེགས་སྤྱིན་པས་ནུབ་ཕྱོགས་ཀྱི་སློབ་མ་རྣམས་ཀྱི་ཆེད་དུ་ནུབ་གླིང་དུ་ཡོད་པའི་བོན་གྱི་འདུས་སྡེ་ཆེན་མོ་དཔལ་གཤེན་བསྟན་དར་རྒྱས་གླིང་དུ་ཕྱི་ལོ་2011ལོར་ཕྱི་ཟླ་01པོའི་ཚེས་15ཉིན་རྫོགས་པར་བྲིས།།

མཁའ་འགྲོ་ཙོ་ཟ་བོན་མོའི་གསོལ་འདེབས།

བསམ་ཡས་ཧས་པོ་རི་ཡི་སྐྱབ་གནས་སུ།
།ཅི་ཡང་མ་ངེས་སྒྱུ་མ་ལྷ་མོའི་སྐུ།
།སྦྱངས་ཤུགས་སྟོབས་ཀྱིས་ལྷག་མེད་མངོན་སངས་རྒྱས།
།རྒྱལ་བའི་យུམ་གྱུར་ཙོ་ཟ་བོན་མོ་ལ།
།དགའ་བདེའི་ངང་དུ་བདག་ཉིད་གསོལ་བ་འདེབས།
།དུས་གསུམ་སངས་རྒྱས་བསྐྱེད་པ་རིན་པོ་ཆེ།
།མཆོག་ཐུན་དངོས་གྲུབ་རྫོགས་པར་བྱིན་གྱིས་རློབས།།
རྫོགས་ཆེན་ཡང་ཀློང་ཆེན་ལས་བྱུར་དུ་ཕྱུང་པ་དགེའོ།།

Lachen Drenpa Namkha

PRAYER TO LACHEN DRENPA NAMKHA

Extracted from *Drenpai Khajang*

ལྷ་ཆེན་དྲན་པ་ནམ་མཁའི་གསོལ་འདེབས་བཞུགས་སོ།།
སྤྲུལ་སྐུ་བློ་ལྡན་སྙིང་པོའི་སྙན་རྒྱུད། སྨན་རིའི་ཡོངས་འཛིན་སློབ་དཔོན་སངས་རྒྱས་བསྟན་འཛིན་གྱིས་དྲན་པའི་
ཁ་བྱང་ལས་ཟུར་དུ་ཕྱུང་བའོ།།

This text is an excerpt from a Khajang prophecy by Drenpa Namkha on the necessities of sentient beings, especially Tibetans. This excerpt was extracted by Yongdzin Rinpoche's Teacher, Menri Lopön Sanggye Tenzin, to read regularly in his daily prayers.

[Visualization]

།།གྱེར་སྤུངས་དྲན་པ་ནམ་མཁའ་ལ།།
GYER PUNG DREN PA NAM KHA LA
Visualize Gyerpung Drenpa Namkha

སྐྱབས་གནས་རྒྱ་མཚོའི་ཚོགས་ཀྱིས་བསྐོར།
KYAB NE GYA TSOI TSOG KYI KOR
Surrounded by oceans of hosts of Refuge Divinities

མངོན་སུམ་མདུན་མཁར་བཞུགས་ནས་ནི།
NGON SUM DÜN KHAR ZHUG NE NI
Actually present in front of you in space.

འབྲལ་མེད་ཐུགས་རྗེས་འཛིན་པར་བསྒོམ།།
DRAL ME THUG JE DZIN PAR GOM
They all behold us unwaveringly in their compassion.

།།ཨེ་མ་ཧོ།།
E MA HO!
Wonderful!

སྐུ་གསུམ་ལྷུན་རྫོགས་ཁོད་སྤུངས་དྲན་པ་མཆོག།
KU SUM LHÜN DZOG KHÖ PUNG DREN PA CHOG
Excellent Khöpung Drenpa who perfectly embodies
the Three Kayas,

ཐུགས་རྗེའི་ལྕགས་ཀྱུས་འགྲོ་ལ་རྟག་འཁྱུད་དེ།
THUG JEI CHAG KYÜ DRO LA TAG KHYU DE
Holding us with the hook of his compassion

ཐུགས་ཀྱི་དམ་བཅའ་གསུང་དུ་བསྒྲགས་པ་ནི།
THUG KYI DAM CHA SUNG DU DRAG PA NI
Thus proclaimed aloud his heartfelt promise:

ང་ཡི་རྗེས་འཇུག་བོན་ལ་མོས་པ་རྣམས།
NGA YI JE JUG BÖN LA MÖ PA NAM
'Whoever follows me and is devoted to Yungdrung Bön

འཇིག་རྟེན་འཁྲུལ་པའི་བྱ་བ་རྒྱབ་ཏུ་བསྐྱུར།
JIG TEN TRUL PAI JA WA GYAB TU KYUR
Should leave the delusion of worldly life behind,

བདེར་གཤེགས་མཛད་སྤྱོད་ཟབ་མོ་ཉམས་སུ་ལོངས།
DER SHEG DZÄ CHYO SAB MO NYAM SU LONG
And practise the profound activities and knowledge of Buddha.

སེམས་ཅན་ཉོན་མོངས་ནད་ཀྱིས་གདུང་བའི་ཚེ།
SEM CHÄN NYON MONG NÄ KYI DUNG WAI TSE
When a sentient being is afflicted by the suffering of sickness and
(disturbing) emotions,

མ་ཡེངས་ང་ལ་གུས་པས་གསོལ་བ་ཐོབ།
MA YENG NGA LA GÜ PE SOL WA THOB
Without distraction, earnestly pray to me with devotion;

ང་ནི་སྨན་ལྷའི་ཚོགས་བཅས་སྡུག་བསྔལ་སེལ།
NGA NI MÄN LHAI TSOG CHE DUG NGAL SEL
I will be a Medicine Buddha surrounded by an entourage and will remove and purify all sufferings and miseries.'

གསུང་པའི་ཞལ་བཞེས་མ་གཡེལ་ཐུགས་རྗེས་གཟིགས།
SUNG PAI ZHAL ZHE MA YEL THUG JE ZIG
Don't forget this promise you made and look upon me with compassion!

རྒྱལ་ཀུན་ངོ་བོ་དྲན་པ་ནམ་མཁའ་མཁྱེན།
GYAL KÜN NGO WO DREN PA NAM KHA KHYEN
You, Drenpa Namkha, who embody all the Buddhas, remember me!

ཐུགས་རྗེས་མཁྱེན་བརྩེ་ནུས་པའི་སྟོབས་ཕྱུང་ལ།
THUG JE KHYEN TSE NÜ PAI TOB CHYUNG LA
Having shown the power of your knowledge, loving-kindness, energy and great compassion,

དུག་ལྔའི་གཅོང་ནད་ཞི་བར་བྱིན་གྱིས་རློབས།
DUG NGAI CHONG NÄ ZHI WAR JYIN GYI LOB
Please bless us so that chronic disease and mental poisons may be pacified!

བར་ཆད་འདྲེ་གདོན་ངན་པས་མནར་བའི་ཚེ།
BAR CHE DRE DÖN NGÄN PE NAR WAI TSE
'When a sentient being is afflicted by sufferings and obstacles caused by evil spirits and ghosts,

མ་ཡེངས་ང་ལ་གུས་པས་གསོལ་བ་ཐོབ།
MA YENG NGA LA GÜ PE SOL WA THOB
Without distraction, earnestly pray to me with devotion;

ང་ནི་ཡི་དམ་ཚོགས་བཅས་བར་ཆོད་སེལ།
NGA NI YI DAM TSOG CHE BAR CHÖ SEL
I will be a yidam surrounded by an entourage and will remove all obstacles.'

གསུང་པའི་ཞལ་བཞེས་མ་གཡེལ་ཐུགས་རྗེས་གཟིགས།
SUNG PAI ZHAL ZHE MA YEL THUG JE ZIG
Don't forget this promise you made and look upon me with compassion!

རྒྱལ་ཀུན་ངོ་བོ་དྲན་པ་ནམ་མཁའ་མཁྱེན།
GYAL KÜN NGO WO DREN PA NAM KHA KHYEN
You, Drenpa Namkha, who embody all the Buddhas, remember me!

ཐུགས་རྗེས་མཁྱེན་བརྩེ་ནུས་པའི་སྟོབས་ཕྱུང་ལ།
THUG JE KHYEN TSE NÜ PAI TOB CHYUNG LA
Having shown the power of your knowledge, loving-kindness, energy and great compassion

འདྲེ་གདོན་བར་ཆོད་ཞི་བར་བྱིན་གྱིས་རློབས།།
DRE DÖN BAR CHÖ ZHI WAR JYIN GYI LOB
Please bless us so that obstacles, evil spirits and ghosts may be pacified!

ཟས་དང་དབུལ་འཕོང་མུ་གེས་གདུང་བའི་ཚེ།
SÄ DANG WUL PHONG MU GE DUNG WAI TSE
'When a sentient being suffers starvation and poverty,

མ་ཡེངས་ང་ལ་གུས་པས་གསོལ་བ་ཐོབ།
MA YENG NGA LA GÜ PE SOL WA THOB
Without distraction, earnestly pray to me with devotion;

ང་ནི་ནོར་ལྷའི་ཚོགས་བཅས་དངོས་གྲུབ་འབེབ།
NGA NI NOR LHAI TSOG CHE NGÖ DRUB BEB
I will be a wealth god surrounded by his entourage and bestow *siddhi*.'

གསུང་པའི་ཞལ་བཞེས་མ་གཡེལ་ཐུགས་རྗེས་གཟིགས།
SUNG PAI ZHAL ZHE MA YEL THUG JE ZIG
Don't forget this promise you made and look upon me with compassion!

རྒྱལ་ཀུན་ངོ་བོ་དྲན་པ་ནམ་མཁའ་མཁྱེན།
GYAL KÜN NGO WO DREN PA NAM KHA KHYEN
You, Drenpa Namkha, who embody all the Buddhas, remember me!

ཐུགས་རྗེས་མཁྱེན་བརྩེ་ནུས་པའི་སྟོབས་ཕྱུང་ལ།
THUG JE KHYEN TSE NÜ PAI TOB CHYUNG LA
Having shown the power of your knowledge, loving-kindness, energy and great compassion

མ་གཡང་ཚོགས་གཉིས་གཏེར་མཛོད་རྒྱས་པར་བྱིན་གྱིས་རློབས།།
MA YENG TSOG NYI TER DZÖ GYE PAR JYIN GYI LOB
Please bless us so that our treasures and prosperity will increase!

ཚེ་ཟད་འཆི་བའི་དུས་ལ་བབ་པའི་ཚེ།
TSE ZÄ CHI WAI DÜ LA BAB PAI TSE
'When a sentient being's life-span is exhausted and he has reached the time of death,

མ་ཡེངས་ང་ལ་གུས་པས་གསོལ་བ་ཐོབ།
MA YENG NGA LA GÜ PE SOL WA THOB
Without distraction, earnestly pray to me with devotion;

ང་ནི་རིག་འཛིན་ཚོགས་བཅས་ཚེ་སྲོག་བསྲིང་།
NGA NI RIG DZIN TSOG CHE TSE SOG SING
I will be Siddha surrounded by an entourage and will extend your life and vital energy.'

གསུང་པའི་ཞལ་བཞེས་མ་གཡེལ་ཐུགས་རྗེས་གཟིགས།
SUNG PAI ZHAL ZHE MA YEL THUG JE ZIG
Don't forget this promise you made and look upon me with compassion!

རྒྱལ་ཀུན་ངོ་བོ་དྲན་པ་ནམ་མཁའ་མཁྱེན།
GYAL KÜN NGO WO DREN PA NAM KHA KHYEN
You, Drenpa Namkha, who embody all the Buddhas, remember me!

ཐུགས་རྗེས་མཁྱེན་བརྩེ་ནུས་པའི་སྟོབས་ཕྱུང་ལ།
THUG JE KHYEN TSE NÜ PAI TOB CHYUNG LA
Having shown the power of your knowledge, loving-kindness, energy and great compassion

ཚེའི་རིག་འཛིན་ཐོབ་པར་བྱིན་གྱིས་རློབས།།
TSE YI RIG DZIN THOB PAR JYIN GYI LOB
Please bless us so that we may become a long-life Rigdzin!

བོན་གྱི་བསྟན་པ་དར་ནུབ་བྱུང་བའི་ཚེ།
BÖN GYI TEN PA DAR NUB JYUNG WAI TSE
'In the turbulent times when the doctrines of Yungdrung Bön wax and wane,

མ་ཡེངས་ང་ལ་གུས་པས་གསོལ་བ་ཐོབ།
MA YENG NGA LA GÜ PE SOL WA THOB
Without distraction, earnestly pray to me with devotion;

ང་ནི་འཕགས་མཆོག་ཚོགས་བཅས་བསྟན་པ་འཛིན།
NGA NI PHAG CHOG TSOG CHE TEN PA DZIN
I will be an excellent exalted one surrounded by my entourage and uphold the Buddha Tönpa Shenrab's doctrines.'

གསུང་པའི་ཞལ་བཞེས་མ་གཡེལ་ཐུགས་རྗེས་གཟིགས།
SUNG PAI ZHAL ZHE MA YEL THUG JE ZIG
Don't forget this promise you made and look upon me with compassion!

རྒྱལ་ཀུན་ངོ་བོ་དྲན་པ་ནམ་མཁའ་མཁྱེན།
GYAL KÜN NGO WO DREN PA NAM KHA KHYEN
You, Drenpa Namkha, who embody all the Buddhas, remember me!

ཐུགས་རྗེས་མཁྱེན་བརྩེ་ནུས་པའི་སྟོབས་ཕྱུང་ལ།
THUG JE KHYEN TSE NÜ PAI TOB CHUNG LA
Having shown the power of your knowledge, loving-kindness, energy and great compassion

གཡུང་དྲུང་བོན་བསྟན་རྒྱས་པར་བྱིན་གྱིས་རློབས།
YUNG DRUNG BÖN TEN GYE PAR JYIN GYI LOB
Please bless us so that the doctrines of Yungdrung Bön may flourish!

བསྟན་འཛིན་གཤེན་པོ་དགྲ་ཡིས་མནར་བའི་ཚེ།
TEN DZIN SHEN PO DRA YI NAR WAI TSE
'When the practitioners who uphold the Teachings are beset by enemies,

མ་ཡེངས་ང་ལ་གུས་པས་གསོལ་བ་ཐོབ།
MA YENG NGA LA GÜ PE SOL WA THOB
Without distraction, earnestly pray to me with devotion;

ང་ནི་སྲུང་མའི་ཚོགས་བཅས་ཀྱི་དྲན་སྒྲོལ།
NGA NI SUNG MAI TSOG CHE GYI DREN DROL
I will be a Guardian surrounded by my entourage and crush all enemies of the doctrines.'

གསུང་པའི་ཞལ་བཞེས་མ་གཡེལ་ཐུགས་རྗེས་གཟིགས།
SUNG PAI ZHAL ZHE MA YEL THUG JE ZIG
Don't forget this promise you made and look upon me with compassion!

རྒྱལ་ཀུན་ངོ་བོ་དྲན་པ་ནམ་མཁའ་མཁྱེན།
GYAL KÜN NGO WO DREN PA NAM KHA KHYEN
You, Drenpa Namkha, who embody all the Buddhas, remember me!

ཐུགས་རྗེས་མཁྱེན་བརྩེ་ནུས་པའི་སྟོབས་ཕྱུང་ལ།
THUG JE KHYEN TSE NÜ PAI TOB CHYUNG LA
Having shown the power of your knowledge, loving-kindness, energy and great compassion

བསྟན་དགྲ་མིང་མེད་ཀླགས་པར་བྱིན་གྱིས་རློབས།
TEN DRA MING ME LAG PAR JYIN GYI LOB
Please bless us so that the enemies of the doctrines may be obliterated!

ལམ་ཞུགས་གང་ཟག་དགེ་སྦྱོར་སྐྱོང་བའི་ཚེ།
LAM ZHUG GANG ZAG GE JYOR KYONG WAI TSE
'When a practitioner who has entered the path carries out the practice of virtues,

མ་གཡེལ་ང་ལ་གུས་པས་གསོལ་བ་ཐོབ།
MA YENG NGA LA GÜ PE SOL WA THOB
Without distraction, earnestly pray to me with devotion;

ང་ནི་མཁའ་འགྲོ་ཚོགས་བཅས་ལུང་རྣམས་སྟོན།
NGA NI KHA DROI TSOG CHE LUNG NAM TÖN
I will be a dakini surrounded by an entourage and
will give you advice.'

གསུང་པའི་ཞལ་བཞེ་མ་གཡེལ་ཐུགས་རྗེས་གཟིགས།
SUNG PAI ZHAL ZHE MA YEL THUG JE ZIG
Don't forget this promise you made and look upon me
with compassion!

རྒྱལ་ཀུན་ངོ་བོ་དྲན་པ་ནམ་མཁའ་མཁྱེན།
GYAL KÜN NGO WO DREN PA NAM KHA KHYEN
You, Drenpa Namkha, who embody all the Buddhas,
remember me!

ཐུགས་རྗེས་མཁྱེན་བརྩེ་ནུས་པའི་སྟོབས་ཕྱུང་ལ།
THUG JE KHYEN TSE NÜ PAI TOB CHYUNG LA
Having shown the power of your knowledge, loving-kindness, energy and great compassion

ཞལ་སྟོན་བོན་གསུང་སྐུ་གསུམ་མངོན་འགྱུར་མཛོད།
ZHAL TÖN BÖN SUNG KU SUM NGÖN GYUR DZÖ
Please show your face and teach us so that we may manifest
the Three Kayas!

ཤི་གསོན་བར་མཚམས་བེམ་རིག་བྲལ་བའི་ཚེ།
SHI SÖN BAR TSAM BEM RIG DRAL WAI TSE
'When a sentient being approaches the moment when body and mind separate between death and life,

མ་གཡེངས་ང་ལ་གུས་པས་གསོལ་བ་ཐོབ།
MA YENG NGA LA GÜ PE SOL WA THOB
Without distraction, earnestly pray to me with devotion;

ང་ནི་བླ་མའི་ཚོགས་བཅས་ངོ་སྤྲོད་མཛད།
NGA NI LA MAI TSOG CHE NGO TRÖ DZÄ
I will be a lama surrounded by an entourage and give you the direct introduction.'

གསུང་བའི་ཞལ་བཞེས་མ་གཡེལ་ཐུགས་རྗེས་གཟིགས།
SUNG WAI ZHAL ZHE MA YEL THUG JE ZIG
Don't forget this promise you made and look upon me with compassion!

རྒྱལ་ཀུན་དྲན་པ་ནམ་མཁའ་མཁྱེན།
GYAL KÜN DREN PA NAM KHA KHYEN
You, Drenpa Namkha, who embody all the Buddhas, remember me!

ཐུགས་རྗེས་མཁྱེན་བརྩེ་ནུས་པའི་སྟོབས་ཕྱུང་ལ།
THUG JE KHYEN TSE NÜ PAI TOB CHYUNG LA
Having shown the power of your knowledge, loving-kindness, energy and great compassion

བར་དོའི་འཁྲུལ་སྣང་ཆོད་པར་བྱིན་གྱིས་རློབས།
BAR DOI THRUL NANG CHÖ PAR JYIN GYI LOB
Please bless us so that all deluded Bardo visions may liberate!

ལྔ་བརྒྱའི་དུས་སུ་ང་ལ་གསོལ་བ་ཐོབ།
NGA GYAI DÜ SU NGA LA SOL WA THOB
'Pray to me with devotion in the time of Kaliyuga;

ང་ནི་བྱིན་རླབས་དགུ་འགྱུར་དེ་དུས་ཆེ།
NGA NI JYIN LAB GU GYUR DE DÜ CHE
The power of my blessings will increase nine-fold at that time.

དུས་བཟང་རྣམས་ལ་བོད་ཁམས་ཡང་ཡང་ཉུལ།
DÜ ZANG NAM LA BÖ KHAM YANG YANG NYUL
I will often come to the realm of Tibet on the special days.

ལས་ཅན་འགའ་ལ་ཞལ་སྟོན་བོན་ཡང་གསུངས།
LE CHÄN GA LA ZHAL TÖN BÖN YANG SUNG
To some qualified ones I will also show my face and teach Bön.

བོད་ཁམས་མཁས་བཙུན་རྣམས་ཀྱི་ཉམས་རྟོགས་ཉུལ།
BÖ KHAM KHE TSÜN NAM KYI NYAM TOG NYUL
I will test the experiences and realization of scholars and practitioners in the realm of Tibet.

ལྔ་བརྒྱ་དྲན་པའི་གྱེར་སྤུངས་དྲན་པ་ང་།
NGA GYA DREN PAI GYER PUNG DREN PA NGA
I am Gyerpung Drenpa Namkha who remembers five hundred (previous lives).

གཤེན་རབ་ཞལ་མཇལ་གསུང་བའི་བོན་རྣམས་ཐོབ།
SHEN RAB ZHAL JAL SUNG WAI BÖN NAM THOB
I have seen Tönpa Shenrab's face and received all his Teachings.

ལོ་ཙའི་ཚིག་སྦྱང་རྒྱ་དཀར་ལན་ལྔ་བྱོན།
LO TSAI TSIG JYANG GYA KAR LÄN NGA JYON
I have learnt language and the art of translation and been to India five times.

རྒྱ་ཞང་རྟག་གཟིགས་བྲུ་ཤ་ཐོད་དཀར་གྱི།
GYA ZHANG TAG ZIG DRU SHA THÖ KAR GYI
I have seen the face of the Siddhas of India, Zhang Zhung, Tagzig, Drusha and Thögar

གྲུབ་ཐོབ་རྣམས་ཀྱི་ཞལ་མཇལ་ཐུགས་བཅུད་ལོན།
DRUB THOB NAM KYI ZHAL JAL THUG CHÜD LÖN
And received their essential Knowledge.

ཚེ་ལ་མངའ་བརྙེས་རིག་འཛིན་གྲལ་དུ་གནས།
TSE LA NGA NYEM RIG DZIN DRAL DU NE
I have taken my place among the ranks of Siddhas and obtained mastery over life.

སྐྱེ་ཤི་མེད་པར་རྒྱུན་དུ་འགྲོ་དོན་མཛད།
KYE SHI ME PAR GYUN DU DRO DON DZÄ
I will always work for the benefit of sentient beings uninterrupted by either death or birth.

ལྔ་བརྒྱའི་དུས་ཀྱི་ཉོན་མོངས་སེམས་ཅན་རྣམས།
NGA GYAI DÜ KYI NYON MONG SEM CHÄN NAM
Sentient beings of the Kaliyuga times who suffer with emotions, pray to me unceasingly with devotion,

མ་ཡེངས་སྙིང་གི་དཀྱིལ་དུ་ང་ཉིད་བསྒོམས།
MA YENG NYING GI KYIL DU NGA NYI GOM
Without distraction, meditate on me at the centre of your heart.

མ་བརྗེ་རྒྱུན་ཆད་མེད་པར་གསོལ་བ་ཐོབ།
MA JE GYUN CHÄ ME PAR SOL WA THOB
Earnestly pray (to me) unceasingly and don't forget me.

མི་འབྲལ་སྤྱི་བོའི་གཙུག་གི་རྒྱན་དུ་ཁུར།
MI DRAL CHYI WOI TSUG GI GYÄN DU KHUR
Cherish me on the crown of your head, as an ornament.

ངས་ནི་ཉེ་རིང་མེད་པར་ཐུགས་རྗེས་བཟུང་།
NGÄ NI NYE RING ME PAR THUG JE ZUNG
I will hold all sentient beings within my compassion, no matter how far or how near they may be.

ཕྱོགས་རིས་མེད་པར་མོས་ཚད་ལམ་སྣ་འདྲེན།
CHYOG RI ME PAR MÖ TSÄ LAM NA DREN
Without bias I will guide all those who are devoted along the path.

རྒྱུན་ཆད་མེད་པར་བྱིན་རླབས་ཆར་ལྟར་འབེབ།
GYUN CHÄ ME PAR JYIN LAB CHAR TAR BEB
I will cause blessings to descend on them like rainfall without ceasing.

འདུ་འབྲལ་མེད་པར་ལུས་དང་སྲོག་ལྟར་སྐྱོབ།
DU DRAL ME PAR LÜ DANG SOG TAR KYOB
I will always protect them as one would one's own life and body.

ཐུགས་རྗེས་ལྕགས་ཀྱུས་གང་མོས་བཟུང་བར་ངེས།
THUG JE CHAG KYU GANG MÖ ZHUNG WAR NGE
With the hook of my compassion I will surely hold whoever has devotion.'

གསུང་པའི་ཞལ་བཞེས་མ་གཡེལ་ཐུགས་རྗེས་གཟིགས།
SUNG PAI ZHAL ZHE MA YEL THUG JE ZIG
Don't forget this promise you made and look upon me with compassion!

རྒྱལ་ཀུན་ངོ་བོ་དྲན་པ་ནམ་མཁའ་མཁྱེན།
GYAL KÜN NGO WO DREN PA NAM KHA KHYEN
You, Drenpa Namkha, who embody all the Buddhas, remember me!

ཐུགས་རྗེས་མཁྱེན་བརྩེ་ནུས་པའི་སྟོབས་བྱུང་ལ།
THUG JE KHYEN TSE NÜ PAI TOB CHYUNG LA
Having shown the power of your knowledge, loving-kindness, energy and great compassion

ཁོད་སྤུངས་ཉིད་དང་དབྱེར་མེད་བྱིན་གྱིས་རློབས།།
KHÖ PUNG NYI DANG YER ME JYIN GIY LOB
Please bless us so that we may become inseparable from you, Khöpung.

ཨ་ཨོཾ་ཧཱུྃ་གྱེར་སྤུངས་དྲན་པ་མུ་ལ་ཉེ་ལོ་ཡོ་ཧཱུྃ་འདུ།

A OM HUNG GYER PUNG DREN PA MU LA NYE LO YO HUNG DU

Orally translated by Yongdzin Lopön Tenzin Namdak Rinpoche
Edited by Khenpo Tenpa Yungdrung, Carol Ermakova and Dmitry Ermakov
Shenten Dargye Ling, 7 August, 2007.